HOW TO
WRITE A LETTER

HOW TO WRITE A LETTER

BY PATRICIA DRAGISIC

A SPEAK OUT, WRITE ON! BOOK
Franklin Watts
A Division of Grolier Publishing
New York / London / Hong Kong / Sydney
Danbury, Connecticut

For permissions for quoted materials see page 122.

Library of Congress Cataloging-in-Publication Data

Dragisic, Patricia.
How to write a letter / by Patricia Dragisic.
p. cm.—(A Speak out, write on! book)
Includes bibliographical references and index.
Summary: Describes the basic parts of many types of business
and personal letters, offers examples of each kind, and suggests ways to
write effectively for particular situations.
ISBN 0-531-11391-4 (lib. bgd.)   0-531-15931-0 (pbk.)
1. Letter writing—Juvenile literature. [1. Letter writing.]
I. Title. II. Series.
PE 1483.D73 1998
808.6—dc21   97-35265
                                        CIP
                                        AC

CONTENTS

HOW TO
WRITE A LETTER

*I*NTRODUCTION

Letter writing is a basic part of life. Being able to write a good letter is a very useful skill, no matter what your age. True, many people don't write to friends anymore—it's so easy just to pick up the telephone and call your friends. But many times, letter writing is important. When you want to look for a job, for example, often the first step is writing a letter to send with your résumé. Also, many good office jobs require that you know how to write letters as part of your work.

If you plan to go to college, you will write a number of letters to various schools to request catalogs, application materials, information, and appointments. As part of the application process, you may need to write to teachers, coaches, employers, and others to request references.

Many finance problems can only be straightened out by letter, not by phone, according to federal law. Even a routine problem such as returning an item and confirming that you've received credit for it requires a letter.

You may keep in touch with your own friends by phone, but you may also have a parent, grandparent, or friend who cannot afford to phone friends around the country (or around the world) very often. If you are asked to write a letter, can you do it and do a good job? Adults may need to write a letter of reference for a friend seeking a job, or for a relative trying to enter the United States. They may turn to you as the one who has a computer at home or at school, or they may turn to you as the one with better writing skills. Can you help them with the important letter they need to write?

One kind of letter that will never go out of style is the love letter. You may be saying to yourself, "I'm not going to use a book to help me write a love letter!" Of course, your personal dreams, feelings, and emotions are just that—very personal. But if you want to put pen to paper to tell that special person just how you feel, you'll be happy that you have put some time into using this book to help you organize your thoughts on paper.

But *is* letter writing going out of style? Some say, "It's the computer age! I send e-mail, not some old-fashioned letter." This book will give you valuable hints on communicating better via electronic messages. Business writers have noticed that e-mail messages are usually shorter and more informal than a letter written on a typewriter or computer. We must learn a whole new set of skills for writing and organizing effective e-mail, and this book teaches those skills.

When you send a letter to anyone, the letter is your personal representative. When you're writing to someone you don't know, as usually happens when you apply for a job, your letter is the only thing the recipient has by which to form an opinion about you— so you'll want to make a good impression, no matter why you're writing. You may be smart and hard-working *and* have great training for a job. If your letter doesn't reflect these points about you, however, the chances that you will get an interview, let alone the job, are very small. This book describes the basic parts of many types of business letters and personal letters and offers examples of each kind to help you decide which letter is best for you.

Investing some time in learning to write letters also brings a return in terms of other forms of communication. Trying to communicate in the form of a letter requires that you organize your thoughts and how you want to express them. That's also what you are doing when you write a book report, a news article for your neighborhood or school newspaper, or a speech. Once you can write a good letter, you have moved ahead in terms of improving your written communications skills for other purposes, too.

There are two ways to see every letter—how it looks and what it says. Let's say that you put together all the thoughts you want to tell someone, but your letter is messy or hard to read. Put yourself in the place of the person who gets that letter. You probably wouldn't be impressed by such a letter or take it seriously. Using this book, you can figure out the right way to write every time!

ONE

WHAT GOES IN YOUR LETTER?

Generations of journalism students have learned to ask and answer a series of questions to write a newspaper article. Writers and reporters do not ask the questions just because "it's always been done that way," but because answering the queries helps them do a good job communicating with their readers. These same questions should be in your mind as you write a letter:

- Who?
- What?
- When?
- Where?
- Why?
- How?
- How much?

Not every question applies to every situation. And it is important to note that you don't need to answer them in any particular order. But if you ask yourself those questions first, and answer them for the reader, chances are good that you have touched on the basic information that people need to know. Look at how confusing it is when a letter writer omits the answer to one of these questions:

Dear All-America Soccer Coaches:

Please come to a meeting of all coaches on Wednesday, January 7, at 7 p.m. We need to plan the championship series for this fall. Coach Esteban Suarez has proposed that we cut down on the number of elimination rounds, to help shorten the season and save money for all the schools.

If you cannot attend, please call Spring Taylor at 555-1234 and let her know. Also, if you will not be at the meeting, please tell Spring whether you are in favor of reducing the number of elimination rounds. Thank you!

Sincerely,
Macho T. Mann

This letter certainly covers anyone's questions about who, what, when, why, and how. But *where* is the meeting?

To help save time for everyone, put all the facts in your letter. In this example, all sixteen coaches in the All-America league may have to call just to find out where the meeting is. Worse yet, many of the coaches may toss the letter aside, intending to call about the place but just not get around to finding out. There goes the meeting and the chance to organize next year's soccer season.

In answering basic questions in your letter, use simple, direct language whenever possible. A letter is not a vocabulary test or a chance to show off those new ten-dollar words you learned last week. Some people think that they need to sound formal or use technical words to convey a message. The best letter—that is, the one that gets results—is easy to read and well written. To review tips that may help you with your letter, see Chapter Six, "Write It Right: Grammar and Word Usage."

PARTS OF A LETTER

Every business letter, and many personal letters, should be set up in a style that answers the reader's questions about you. See the sample on page 19 for details. Begin with your return address and the date. Next comes the address, including the postal ZIP code, of the person you are writing to.

Then you fill in the salutation, or the line that says "Dear So-and-so." When you are writing a letter looking for a job, or any business letter to someone you don't know yet, it's best to be businesslike and address them as "Dear Mr. Smith" or "Dear Dr. Curezit." Let's say you get that great job at the senior center and write letters regularly to Ms. Betty Bureaucrat at the state's office of aging. The first time you write to her, it's polite to address her as "Dear Ms. Bureaucrat" in the salutation. After you write to her a couple of times and talk to her on the phone, it might be perfectly acceptable and normal then to begin your letters "Dear Betty."

The body of your letter contains as many paragraphs as it needs to say what you need to say. This is the information, the heart of the matter—why you are writing the letter.

Then there is a complimentary close, such as "Sincerely," "Very truly yours," or "Cordially." Most people use "Sincerely" or "Very truly yours" for a business letter to someone they haven't met yet or don't know well. For example, "Sincerely" is always a good way to end a letter applying for a job. "Cordially" is an upbeat and positive complimentary close to use on letters to those people you like and work well with. (It means "warmly," or, more literally, from the heart.)

Then you leave four lines of space for your written signature, and type your name below that. Just in case your handwriting is not the clearest on the planet, the person will still know how to spell your name when he or she writes back to you.

For business letters, and some kinds of personal letters, you may also add a "cc" list, or copies' list, after you type your name. Originally "cc" stood for "carbon copies." People no longer use carbon paper to make a copy of a letter or other document; instead, they photocopy the letter or print an extra copy on the computer. But you'll still want to send copies of some letters to other people, and you designate those after the letters "cc:" (with a colon and then a space or two before the first name listed).

A FORMAT FOR YOUR LETTER

Anyone who has used WordPerfect or Microsoft Word software for a computer is familiar with the term "format." It refers to the way you set up your document to look, including margins on the top, bottom, and sides; amount of space between lines (single-spacing or double-spacing); the typeface you use; and the use of page numbers and other features. Whether you are using a typewriter or computer software to write your letter, you still need to think about and set up a format as you start.

PARTS OF A LETTER:

return address and date

123 Ida B. Wells Drive
Bronx, NY 00000
January 7, 1999

name and address (including ZIP)

Harry Arms
Director of Admissions
Delta Business College
123 Michael Jordan Drive
Raleigh, NC 00000

body of letter

Dear Mr. Arms: salutation

Enclosed is my application for the hospitality management program at your college. I really want to go to Delta to help my brother with his catering business. He already makes the world's best enchiladas, tacos, guacamole, and other food. But he and I both think the business needs the type of background I could get from your program.

When we talked recently, you asked that I include the name of a reference, someone who knows me well from school or work. Please write to Velvet Voice, Assistant Principal, Joe's High School, 456 Joe Boulevard, Bronx, NY 00000. Ms. Voice is our faculty adviser at the candy sale at school.

I look forward to hearing from you soon.

Sincerely, complimentary close

Marianna Islands your typed name

cc: Velvet Voice list of people to receive copies

Most teachers and employers today are flexible about margins at the top, bottom, left, and right of your document. If you write on a typewriter, it's important to remember that you shouldn't type too close to the bottom of the paper; this is sloppy and difficult to photocopy. Also, if your letter is extremely short (one or two short paragraphs) it will look better if you add some additional space at the top above or below your return address, so that the letter does not look crowded onto the top part of the page. You might also be able to use a document layout feature to center the text vertically, that is, with equal space above and below the letter on the page.

The samples here are single-spaced. If your employer asks you to draft a letter for him or her to edit, it's usually a good idea to make the lines double-spaced, so that the boss has room to make corrections or add comments. To emphasize that it's a draft, stamp or write in red "draft" at the top of the first page.

The sample letter also shows double-spacing between paragraphs; this makes your letter easier to read. Most businesses today use block style or modified block style. In block style, you do not indent the first line of each paragraph. You position all the major elements of your letter (date, name and address, text, complimentary close, and typed signature) flush left, as shown in the letter on page 21. In modified block style, the date, your return address (if you are not writing on letterhead stationery) and complimentary close and typed signature may be indented to the center of your paper. For a sample of modified block style, see the letter on page 22.

BLOCK STYLE:

October 16, 1998

Evelyn Chang Lee
111 Prairie Drive
Iowa City, Iowa 00000
(515) 563-0749

China Seas Fortune Cookies, Ltd.
111 Harvey Milk Drive
San Francisco, California 90000

Dear China Seas:

Thank you for your letter notifying us that there will be a delay in shipping our order of 750 fortune cookies (series 2C: adult themes) that we need by November 5. If we pay extra for express shipping, is there a possibility that you can still meet the date of our class reunion, November 5?

Please call me at the above number to let us know about express shipping and what it costs for an order of this amount.

Sincerely,

Evelyn Chang Lee

MODIFIED BLOCK STYLE:

CHINA SEAS FORTUNE COOKIES, LTD.
111 HARVEY MILK DRIVE,
SAN FRANCISCO, CALIFORNIA 90000

November 12, 1998

Ms. Evelyn Chow Lee
111 Prairie Drive
Iowa City, Iowa 00000

Dear Ms. Lee:

Thank you for your recent letter to my supervisor, complimenting me for expediting the shipment of your rush order of fortune cookies. You and several other people were thoughtful enough to return the postcard providing feedback on service with positive comments about me. As a result, I received a bonus check.

We are sorry that your minister was offended by the adult themes in the fortune cookies. We offer adult themes for showers, bachelor parties, "roasts," and reunions. If you still have our catalog on hand, you'll note that we give several examples of adult-type messages to help our customers avoid embarrassing surprises. We hope you will still be a customer in the future; perhaps you'll want to consider an order of series 3A: Positive Inspiration messages, for your next church event.

Yours very truly,

John Doe

HOW TO PICK A TYPEFACE

Part of your message when you communicate is how your letter looks. The typeface you use is an important part of how the reader sees your letter. Sometimes you don't have a choice of type. Most electric typewriters use one typeface only, although there is one popular brand that uses a rotating metal ball which contains all the letters. The rotating metal ball can be switched to change the typeface. Some electronic word processors, which are halfway between a typewriter and a computer, offer only one kind of type. With most computers, however, there is a range of typefaces available to you.

Often the choice of type is a personal matter, and many of the faces that are available on a computer are appropriate for you to use. Consider some special typefaces that you have probably noticed, whether you think you are aware of type styles or not. For example, gothic type is often used for invitations to Halloween events and for some kinds of music shows; note these examples:

WORLD'S COOLEST HALLOWEEN PARTY!

CONCERT by Nightshade Nail Twisters

If you or a family member has ever ordered personalized stationery through a catalog or department store mailing, you may have noticed that a few type styles seem especially popular. A graceful, flowing script designed to look like handwriting may seem suitable for a party invitation. A bolder style might seem right for a memo pad. A fanciful or childlike style might be appropriate for a humorous newsletter.

The point is that you can exercise creativity in choosing type to use on posters, invitations, and many types of personal letters. But it's good to stick with the tried-and-true when you are writing a business letter, especially a cover letter with a résumé when you are looking for a job. Some people, aware that there are usually many applicants for every job, think that they need to make their letters stand out or look visibly different to get the attention of the person hiring. Usually, however, the employer is looking for someone who can fit into his or her organization, rather than someone who has simply found an offbeat typeface.

TYPE WITH OR WITHOUT SERIFS

There are two broad groups of type, and within these two broad groups are many individual typefaces. The first group is made up of types with serifs, which are the small extenders on letters such as "r," "t," and "y." The sample letters in this book are set in Times Roman, a type with serifs. Many people believe that those extenders on the letters make it easier for our eyes to read easily across a line, so this fairly traditional style of type remains common.

The other broad group of typefaces are considered more contemporary. This is the sans-serif group, which eliminates those extenders on the letters. ("Sans" is French for "without.") This book uses Helvetica Light, a sans-serif type. Here's another example of sans-serif type:

Anxiety today: any progress?

Many students like sans-serif type, when they have access to it, for their homework and personal correspondence. They think it is cleaner or crisper looking and gives an up-to-date impression. In business, however, it is smart to ask the employer his or her preference or consult the company's style sheet (which lists the standard format for many kinds of documents), if there is one.

THE SIZE OF YOUR TYPE

Again, you don't always have a choice. But if you're working on a computer, you can change the size of the type when formatting your document. A good rule of thumb is to save larger sizes of type for display materials such as posters, ads, and invitations.

Most businesses use 10-point, 11-point, or 12-point type for the text of letters. The point system of measuring type was developed by printers before computers were invented; a point is 1/72 of an inch. A capital letter in 12-point type, then, is 1/6 of an inch (4.25 mm) tall. On a computer, it is easy to view the letter in different type sizes and decide what size is best before printing the document.

ADVANCED FORMAT: ONE LETTER TO MANY DIFFERENT PEOPLE

If you want to send the same letter to many people, you have a couple of options. One is to use a general salutation, such as "Greetings," and omit the individual's address from the letter itself. See, for example, the letter to the All-America Soccer Coaches on page 16. You can photocopy the more general letter for all sixteen people, and then you just need to type the names and addresses onto the envelopes. This is acceptable for many kinds of letters that you send or receive as a volunteer—for example, letters from school clubs, community centers, amateur sports groups, community religious groups, block clubs, and arts groups.

In business, however, it is considered too casual to send the same letter to sixteen people, addressing them all as "Dear Major Mogul." But you do not need to retype the same letter sixteen times if you are working on a computer. You can use a "mail merge" feature that enables you to use your body text as the first document, a list of names and addresses (including salutations) as a second document, and the mail-merge feature to create the sixteen letters that you need. See the manual for the word processing software that you use for instructions on how to use the mail-merge feature.

PICKING YOUR PAPER

For business, especially for résumés and cover letters applying for a job, it is best to stick with the proven favorite colors: white or off-white. Use standard-sized business paper (often labeled as typing paper), which is 8-1/2 by 11 inches. Odd sizes of paper may look interesting or pleasing to the eye but are difficult to stack for photocopying or filing.

When writing a cover letter to apply for a job, some people—once again, conscious of a large group of competing applicants—think that they might help their letter or résumé stand out by using lime-green or purple paper. This is an urge to resist! Colorful papers are fun but not businesslike.

LETTERHEAD AND LOOKING SHARP

Suppose you get that job you applied for, whether it is part-time while you are in school or full-time after graduation. If your job involves letter writing, you will probably be expected to use the company's letterhead. This is stationery with the company's name, address, and phone numbers already printed on it.

Here are a few thoughts to keep in mind when you use letterhead:

- Do a draft of your letter on plain white paper first and proofread it, or present it to your supervisor for his or her approval as requested, before going to letterhead. This saves money: Letterhead is usually a heavier, more expensive grade of paper than the white paper normally used for printouts.

- Line up, or align, the left margin of your document to align with the letterhead. If your text is too far to the left or right of the type on your letterhead, the resulting letter looks unprofessional and sloppy. Note these examples:

Poor alignment, or lack of alignment at the left margin:

Jane Austen Memorabilia
234 Literature Lane
Anglophile, Pennsylvania 10400
Telephone: 213-555-1212

Professor Peter Piper
Chair, English Department
Earnest Community College
Earnest, Oklahoma 80888

Dear Professor Piper:

Good alignment (nice use of letterhead!):

Jane Austen Memorabilia

234 Literature Lane
Anglophile, Pennsylvania 10400
Telephone: 213-555-1212

Professor Peter Piper
Chair, English Department
Earnest Community College
Earnest, Oklahoma 80888

Dear Professor Piper:

Using letterhead stationery might sometimes affect the content of your letter slightly. As in the above example, if you want to ask Professor Piper to call you, you can include in your letter a line that says, "If you have any questions, or want to discuss any of the proposals I have outlined, please give me a call any morning at the above number." But, if you are writing a letter for a business that just got a new fax machine and there is no fax number on the letter-head stationery you are using, remember to include the fax number: "If you want to fax your order in the future, the number for our new fax machine is 213-555-2121."

Letterhead stationery is useful not only to convey a certain image about you or your organization, but it also provides information that the person or company you are writing to may need. As long as you keep in mind what information is and is not included in the letterhead, you are doing your best to communicate via letter.

THE ENVELOPE: PART OF A PACKAGE

Let's imagine that you have finished your letter and checked it over. You are satisfied with what it says and how it looks; this letter represents you well! Is anything missing? Yes, you also need to produce an envelope that will get the letter to its correct destination quickly and that also reflects how well you communicate.

A standard-sized envelope is a business envelope that measures about 4-1/4 by 9-1/2 inches (11 by 24 cm). It is best to use a white business envelope for your business correspondence and many types of personal letters, such as letters to the editor (see next chapter). For personal letters to friends and family, you can choose envelopes from a wide range of papers, colors, and sizes.

In the upper left corner of the envelope, write or type your return address, starting with your name. Always include your own 5-digit postal ZIP code. The "ZIP + 4" code pinpoints your address more closely for the US Postal Service. This information is then handy when the person decides to write back to you. Also, if the person you are writing to has moved, or if the address is incorrect, the Postal Service may return the letter to you, and that process will be delayed if you have omitted your ZIP code.

Just about in the middle of the envelope, write or type the name and address (again including ZIP code) of the person to whom you are writing. If one line of the address is exceptionally long, break that line at some logical point and indent the remainder of it two to five spaces on the next line. This helps avoid running the address off the right edge of the envelope. Here's an example:

Professor Luke Skywalker
Foundation for the Advancement of
    Science Fiction in Literature
1000 Asimov Boulevard
Bradbury, WA 90000

If you use a computer, consult your manuals to see if you can print address labels with the hardware and software available to you.

TWO

PERSONAL LETTERS: "DEAR WORLD"

Some people think of the personal letter, if they think of it at all, as extinct, like the dinosaur or the home without a color television set. Yet, despite the lure of the telephone, there are many times when a personal letter is your best choice for expressing yourself. A personal letter can be very informal and brief. For some types of personal letters, however, it is best to keep a few rules in mind to help you communicate effectively.

LETTERS TO THE EDITOR

You may feel strongly about an issue and decide to write a letter to the editor of your school newspaper or to the daily or weekly newspaper in your city or town. Or you may be involved in a club or community group that asks you to write a letter to the editor to get the group's opinion on record.

There are two simple tests of whether your letter to the editor is effective. The first is whether the editor of the newspaper selects it to appear in the paper, and the second is whether the readers of the newspaper understand your letter and are influenced by it.

Here are some guidelines that may help you get the editor's attention. Some of this advice is based on my experience in getting letters published, and a lot of it is based on common sense:

- Be brief. Space is limited in most letters to the editor sections or columns. The editor of the paper is looking for an offbeat subject or an unusual angle to a story that a lot of people are writing about. No one has time to wade through pages of your opinions, however interesting or informed they may be.

- Get to the point fast. Rather than going through a big buildup on an issue and then stating your main point as a conclusion, be sure to state the main point in your first sentence or paragraph. This keeps the casual reader from losing interest or getting confused.

- Be specific. If you are writing to a Los Angeles newspaper, but your letter is about the mayor of a suburb, be sure to specify that to avoid confusion: "Mayor Ralph Rabblerouser of Paradise Beach has been criticized for. . . ."

- Be polite and respectful. Even if you are writing to contradict another opinion published in the paper, or to challenge a statement by a public figure, you need to tame your intense feelings about the topic as part of the communication process. The editor will not need (and readers will not heed) opinions expressed in an insulting way. Always turn your thoughts around to ask yourself how you would feel if someone wrote about you, your family, or your community group in terms like those you want to use!

- Mention sources for your information. Don't just say that Mayor Rabblerouser's spending on his campaign exceeded normal limits. What are normal limits and who says so? For example: "According to a Government and Politics Foundation report published in *Newsguy*, a mayoral candidate for a city of this size spends $100,000 to $250,000 on his or her campaign; Mayor Rabblerouser spent ten times more."

Following is an example of a letter to the editor discussing whether taxes should be raised to increase funding for community libraries. Note that the writer is aware of the fact that many readers will not agree with him, but he does not adopt a defensive tone. Trying to change the perspectives in a debate or argument is a classic way to approach a controversial topic.

Letters to the Editor Section
Banana Bay Bugle
123 Peel Street
Banana Bay, AR 00000

To the Editor:

The junior English classes at Plantain High have gotten together to urge voters to support the 1.5-cent increase in property taxes (for each $10,000 of assessed value). The money raised by this tax increase will go to help the Banana Bay public library system. With the funds to be raised by the tax increase, the library system will be able to afford two new computers for each of the branch libraries. In addition, the main library can afford to stay open every weekday evening, not just two evenings.

As students, we use the library regularly for homework assignments. Some Banana Bay residents may say that they do not want to pay the tax because their children are out of school and do not use the libraries. Twenty students from our classes visited the main library regularly for three weeks to collect information on the type of activities there. We learned that about 20 percent of the programs were targeted to senior citizens, including Elderhostel classes and a series of lectures on "Arthritis and Joint Replacement: What Are the Facts?"

Also, the busiest section is the Business and Commerce library, and the average age of patrons in that section is well over 30. Librarians in Business and Commerce told us that most people who ask for reference help are looking for information on companies that will help them find new jobs, or they are looking for material that will help them improve their businesses or streamline their work. The entire community benefits from the library system, and we hope everyone will vote to continue the community support of libraries.

Sincerely,

LETTERS TO A PUBLIC OFFICIAL

Sometimes you feel strongly about an issue and decide to write to your congressional representative, senator, or other public official to express your opinion. It is your right as a voter, or future voter, to take a stand and to attempt to influence the way your representative will vote in a legislative session. There is no guarantee that your letter will influence your representative; he or she may reply that conscience is an important factor or that the community gave some discretion to the representative in the process of electing him or her. But if you don't even try to make your viewpoint known, how can you complain when your representative votes against what you want?

Many of the informal rules for letters to the editor also work well for this type of letter. Your letter is most likely to have an impact if it is brief and to the point, respectful in tone, and factual whenever that is appropriate. If you are writing in response to a speech that you heard on television, it is helpful to mention that as a source. It is also good common sense to mention that you live in the representative's district or perhaps that your family has been living and voting in the district for many years. Also, if your family has supported or worked for candidates in the senator's party, that's useful to mention.

You may or may not get a reply letter. Usually, when you write to a congressional representative in the US House, or to your US Senator, you get a form letter in reply. The form letter was written to anticipate the many letters your representative expects to receive. Sometimes this seems disappointing, but remember that your chances of establishing a personal correspondence with a busy public official are slim. Your real goal should be to influence a vote.

Where do you get the names and addresses of various public officials? Try your school library or your local public library. The librarian can tell you which officials represent which towns or communities and can look up the addresses for your state capitol or for the US Congress.

THANK-YOU NOTES

One of the biggest contradictions in the universe is that everyone likes to receive gifts, but most people hate to write thank-you notes! This is another type of letter writing in which it is most helpful to put yourself in the other person's position. You like the fact that Aunt Shirley sends you gifts on your birthday and for the holidays, but doesn't she understand that you're really too busy to write a thank-you note? No, she doesn't understand that, and if you don't write, eventually good old Aunt Shirley will figure you didn't care about her gift packages, and she'll stop sending them.

Etiquette writers usually advise a handwritten note on plain note paper. If you feel comfortable only with typing on a computer, then a computer-generated letter is better than no letter. Some people who are reminded to write letters think that it is OK to substitute a thank-you card and just sign their names, but again, put yourself in Aunt Shirley's shoes. Would she appreciate more than just your name on a card? Of course she would.

Your thank-you note should have at least two sentences in it. The first should be along the lines of "thanks very much for thinking of me with this gift." The second should mention something specific you liked about the gift. (A printed card that says "thank you for your gift" doesn't reveal if you even remember what the gift was.)

A personal thank-you letter is an informal note, so you don't need to put the person's name and address on the letter as you would for a letter to the editor or a letter to your representative. Also, for this type of personal letter, you use a comma after the salutation ("Dear So-and-so"), rather than a colon. This sample thank-you letter will give you an idea of how to let Aunt Shirley know you appreciate her thoughtfulness (and should help keep those gifts coming):

Dear Aunt Shirley,

Thank you very much for sending me a Chicago Bulls sweatshirt. As you know, I am really a fan of the Bulls and hope to be able to attend one of their games in person someday. Our biology class is planning a nature walk this fall, and it will be cool to wear a Bulls shirt to stay warm!

We all hope to see you soon.

Love,
Elvis, Jr.

SYMPATHY LETTERS

As with the thank-you letter, you can just go out and buy a printed sympathy card. A letter, though, is a more personal way to express your support for a friend or acquaintance who has suffered the death of a family member or close friend. If you knew the person who died, remember to include a sentence or two mentioning what you liked about him or her—or recalling some significant occasion that you spent together. If you did not feel close to the person who died, this is not the time to mention it; in such a case, you can mention the fact that you know how much your friend will miss the loved one.

To make sure that your letter helps or is a nice gesture, remember that the purpose is to express sympathy in a positive way for the living person who has lost someone from his or life. This is *not* a time to play medical reporter and say something like, "Everyone agreed the case was hopeless, and he was sick so long; it's all for the best." Imagine receiving a letter like this, and you can see that it's not comforting and does not speak to your feelings of loss or sadness!

This sample letter incorporates the above ideas of trying to make the survivor feel better while addressing your memories of the person who has died:

Dear Darius,

I was so sorry to hear that your father died, and at such a young age. We all remember how he showed up for all the Boy Scout hikes and outdoor expeditions and helped us find the trails. He always tried to be a leader and care about all the kids. See you soon at school.

Your friend,
Dion

NOTES OF APOLOGY

A brief note with a couple of sentences can help you smooth over some awkward situations. When you need to say you're sorry, and it's difficult to call the person to talk about it, consider a letter of apology. As in a sympathy note, be honest, but not critical or negative. You don't need to "crawl" or grovel, but neither do you want to keep an argument going. Try to be positive and say what you need to, no more and no less.

Consider this example:

Dear Mr. Soldes,

I'm sorry that we broke the window in your store on Monday. It was nice of your nephew Hector to say that he did it, but I was the one batting. Here is a check for $30 to help replace the window. My mom suggested that if that's not enough money, maybe I could work for you after school a couple of days to make up the difference. Please let me know. You can call her or me at 321-5555.

Sincerely,
Joe Castro

LETTERS OF INVITATION

You can buy printed cards for many occasions at a card store or drugstore, but it's nice to be able to write a personalized letter or note inviting people to a party or reception. Be sure to include answers to all the basic questions mentioned in Chapter One—*who, what, when, where,* and *why*. (*How* and *how much* may not always need to be included.) You can write your invitation out in sentence form, like any other note, or you can center each of the lines in an artistic fashion; see the following example:

Please come to a reception
in honor of Coach Susan Washington
and the Girls' Basketball Team
Saturday, June 20,
4 p.m. at the North Fieldhouse

(shh! it's a surprise for the coach)

FAN LETTERS

You may have the urge to write a letter to your favorite musician or actor to tell him or her how much you like his or her work, and how much a favorite song, film, or TV series means to you. All stars love to get fan mail, but to keep your letter positive for you and for the person you're writing to, here are some informal rules to keep in mind:

- Keep your letter short—one page at the most.

- Don't enclose a gift; Sammie Z. Star will probably never see it or be able to appreciate it.

- Don't ask for a phone call or an appointment to visit. Exception: if the person is an actor on a TV series performed before a studio audience, you can ask for information on how to get tickets for a certain date (at least a month in advance).

If you are writing to request a photo, state that clearly. Some recording companies and TV or film production companies send out free pictures of their stars as part of their normal publicity program. In other cases, a secretary will send you a form to order a photo or other memorabilia such as T-shirts, and payment will be required. Or you may be sent the name and address of a fan club for that star, and the club will charge a membership fee or ask for a separate payment for a photo.

How do you get the address of your favorite star? For a recording star, read the information on the label for the audiocassette or compact disc (CD). Sometimes there will be a separate address provided for the singer, musician, or group. If not, write to Sammie Z. Star "c/o Starflight Music" at the address provided on the cassette or CD. You might find an Internet address for the home page of the performer or the record company; go to that web site to find a mailing address. For a television or film star, write down the name of the production company at the end of a show, and go to your local library to get the address of the production company.

REQUESTS FOR INFORMATION

At the end of a newspaper or magazine article, you may find a notice indicating that you can get more information on the subject you've been reading about by writing to XYZ agency or association. You may be writing a report on environmental issues, for example, and could use authoritative information from or about an environmental organization.

Remember to keep your letter brief and as specific as possible. For example, if you are writing to an environmental organization, don't ask for "any information about the environment." That's too general and too broad. Are you interested in air pollution, water quality, on saving some endangered animal species? Mention your particular concern if you have one.

Many organizations are committed to outreach programs and prepared to supply information. But many government agencies and nonprofit organizations have been through budget-cutting crises and may not have the staff or resources to answer your queries in detail. So don't just assume that by writing a letter you can get someone you don't know to do your homework for you! The *Encyclopedia of Associations* is a reference work that you may find at your school library or public library; it lists addresses for many types of organizations and often notes whether the group provides information to the public.

Wherever you find the address, make a point of noticing if the organization asks for a self-addressed stamped envelope ("SASE") to save on its postage costs. If so, put your name and address on a full-sized business envelope as the addressee, and don't forget the stamp.

LETTER TO TOURIST AGENCY

Most countries and all the fifty states in the United States operate tourist offices or agencies and provide information to encourage you to visit and spend your travel dollars there. Often these tourist agencies have a lot of good free information available, including calendars of events, maps, and other information geared to your interests. In the travel section of your newspaper (usually a Sunday feature in most cities), you'll see ads from nearby states or from countries that have some hopes of attracting people from your area.

Often you can call for information, but what if you're busy during the day when the office is open, or if the line is always busy when you do have a chance to call? Assuming that you have plenty of time (six weeks or two months) before a possible trip, write a brief letter explaining specifically what you're interested in. You'll probably get more useful information if you say, for example, that you're interested in visiting Michigan in the fall and you're particularly interested in cross-country skiing and downhill skiing.

To find the address of a tourist agency "cold"—without an ad right in front of you—ask your local library for assistance.

COMPLAINING TO A MANUFACTURER

Let's say you buy a new portable radio with headphones, and it comes with a thirty-day warranty or guarantee. A week or two after the warranty expires, you notice that the stations are "drifting," that you do not get clear reception anywhere. Chances are that the store where you purchased the item will say you're out of luck because the warranty is expired. Another option then is to write to the manufacturer and ask that the item be replaced.

State the facts clearly and simply, and again, keep your letter short. Be careful not to be abusive or use insulting language. Picture yourself or one of your family members reading a letter filled with sarcastic insults—you would not be inclined to help a person who sent such a letter.

Anything positive that you can say as part of your presentation is probably a good idea to help get your request taken seriously. Review this sample letter with an eye towards adapting it to your situation, noting the first sentence especially:

June 26, 1998

Happy Electronics, Ltd.
777 Stereo Blvd.
Rahway, NJ 00000

Dear Happy Electronics:

My family has always been satisfied with radios and CD players made by your company, and we have owned several different models. Recently, however, I was disappointed by the Joggers' Jiggle-Free X99 model radio with headphones that I bought with my birthday money. I can't run or even walk while wearing this unit. Shortly after the warranty expired, I found that even sitting quietly in the park, I could not get clear reception on any stations.

I tried tuning in to all the big 50,000-watt stations in our town, thinking that a station with more broadcast power would work better. I did check the batteries and the connection from the radio to the headset, and that was all fine.

Because the radio is so new, and because I expect better quality from a Happy product, I ask that you provide me with a replacement unit. Please advise how I can get the replacement unit. Thank you.

Sincerely,
Joe Junior

HOLIDAY LETTERS

Many families do not have the time to send individual greetings at Christmas or Hannukah to all their friends, relatives, and neighbors, and they prefer to send a form letter prepared on the computer. This is another type of letter that your parents may be interested in writing, but they turn to you as a computer-friendly person to put it together for the family.

It's easy to make fun of these letters, and many good writers have done so! The writers often brag too much, or they include too much depressing personal information. "We're so pleased and proud that Keisha won the Nobel Prize and Harrington discovered a cure for cancer. But here's a tragic note: Grandma just keeps suffering with that new partial plate that doesn't fit; her dentist won't even help her!" This is exaggeration (I hope!) as an example of what no one expects to read.

Your letter can be warm, friendly, full of updates, and enjoyable to all those who get it. Again, as with so many other types of letters, don't write too much. If you have graphics available, it's fun to add one or two to the letter. Colored paper will make your greetings cheery, and if you have time, write a few words at the top or bottom of the form letter: "Hi Allen, See you in February at the meeting."

LOVE LETTER OR VALENTINE NOTE

It's simple: Write from the heart, and your love letter or love note will be better than any printed greeting card. Most people still prefer a more personal handwritten letter to a typed or computer-generated letter. Don't write anything intimate if you will be handing the letter to someone in a school situation or if you haven't actually dated the person yet. If your love letter is an apology for something, keep that brief. Do not imagine that anger is part of a genuine love letter. Your aim is to let the other person know you care, and you want him or her to value your letter and keep it as a treasured possession.

THREE

BUSINESS LETTERS—GETTING A FOOT IN THE DOOR

Knowing how to write a good business letter is one of the keys to getting a better education and a better job. Try to make your letter as brief as possible while still making the points you need to make. Remember that time is at a premium for most people today. You may have some fascinating stories to tell in a job interview, but you do not need to include them in your cover letter. You greatly increase your chances of having your letter taken seriously if you state your points directly and in a well-organized format.

To start writing business letters, review the seven questions—*who, what, when, where, why, how,* and *how much*—in Chapter One. If your letter answers any and all of these questions that are relevant to your situation, you are well on your way to writing an effective business letter.

A note about tone: Treating others with respect is smart in any business letter, so that you can be respected and treated seriously in turn. Do not use slang expressions such as "way cute" in a business letter. Most experts advise that you do not include contractions such as "isn't" or "we've," but that instead you spell out "is not" or "we have." You may personally believe that this is a minor point, because you are smart and have a lot to offer. Nevertheless, just as you expect people to behave in a certain way if they visit your school or home, the people to whom you are sending your letters have ideas about how you should communicate to meet their needs.

Neatness counts. A business letter with smudges, crossed-out or written-in information, or strikeovers in typing does not make a good impression. Again, you may think that a neat letter does not really matter because your thoughts are so profound. But with many people applying for the same job or to the same college, how do you make your letter look good? The answer is by making it neat and professional-looking.

APPLYING TO A COLLEGE OR VOCATIONAL SCHOOL

Most students are relieved to find that an application to a college or vocational school is a form for you to fill out, with questions such as the name of your high school or community college and names and addresses of people who will give you references. This is a "fill-in-the-blanks" process once you locate all the information, such as the complete address of Uncle Dan, your father's friend from military service who is now mayor of a nearby town. Often, however, you are asked to submit a letter or essay explaining why you want to attend a particular school, what you have learned at school so far besides the subject matter taught in the courses on your transcript, why the school should choose you over someone else, and what your goals for the future are.

If you are asked to supply this information, your best chance of making a good impression on the admitting officer is to write a letter on a computer or typewriter. Read the instructions carefully to see if the essay should be on a separate sheet of paper or must be typed into a space provided on the application form (or if you are specifically asked to write out your thoughts in your own handwriting). Address each question with specific examples of things you have done, rather than with adjectives ("excellent" or "really terrific," for example) to make the best impression. Here are a couple of examples of how to answer the question of why the school should choose you over someone else:

- For the past two years, I have learned responsibility and how to organize my time by working 20 hours a week for the park district while maintaining a B average.

- During the current school year, I am president of the career club and secretary of the Junior Achievement chapter; my guidance counselor calls that leadership in action.

COVER LETTER IN REPLY TO AN AD FOR A JOB

So the big day has arrived, and you are ready to look for a job. Like most people, you will probably start your search by looking at the help-wanted classified ads in the newspapers in your town, or in the town where you want to work. Often the ad will state something like "résumés to this address." So do you even need a cover letter? Yes, you need a cover letter, for at least a couple of reasons. The cover letter shows that you are willing to go that extra mile to make a good impression. Also, if your qualifications are light in some areas mentioned in the ad, you can use the cover letter to put a positive spin on that information, in a straightforward, nondefensive manner.

Begin your cover letter by mentioning the ad you are answering, and summarize or explain your qualifications as set out in the ad. Then, describe *how* the prospective employer can contact you to set up an interview. If you are currently employed and cannot receive calls where you work, ask the recruiter to call you at home and leave a message on your voice mail or answering machine. If you can receive calls at your current workplace, note that you can take calls at that number on a confidential basis during business hours.

See the letter below as a possible reply to an ad for an Editorial Assistant who types at least 50 words per minute, knows certain word processing programs, has used proofreading symbols, and is willing to do clerical work in addition to editorial tasks:

99 Lake Shore Drive
Chicago, IL 60600
October 28, 1998

Box 1234
New York Big Bugle
123 Hobnob Highway
Importantville, Long Island,
New York 10400

Dear *New York Big Bugle*:

In response to your recent ad in the *Chicago Gazette*, I would like to apply for the position of Editorial Assistant with your newspaper. For the past two years, I have worked as an editor on the sports section of our college newspaper, the *Student Standard*, where I learned to write and edit on a computer under deadline pressure, to proofread, and to love journalism.

Please see my enclosed résumé, which also mentions the 36 hours of English courses I have completed in college. It's hard to communicate enthusiasm on a résumé; however, I consider myself a team player and a hard worker ready to take on all the everyday jobs that will help your editorial team move forward.

I look forward to the opportunity of a personal interview, and I plan to be in New York visiting my sister the week of November 26. Please leave a message on my phone machine at the dorm, where my number is 773-555-0000. Thank you.

Sincerely,
Sammy Sidelines

COVER LETTER APPLYING FOR A JOB WHERE YOUR FRIEND WORKS

You may be in the fortunate position of knowing someone who works at a company or organization that might have a place for you. Also, you may then have the opportunity to hear about job openings from your friend or relative before they are advertised. If a friend tells you about a possible opening, make sure that the person feels comfortable about recommending you before you sit down to write your letter. That is, do not use the person's name without permission, as the personnel department or prospective supervisor may call the person directly to ask him or her about you. Here's a sample of the type of letter you might use; note that it's in your best interest to position yourself for many different types of job openings, not just the one in your friend's department.

555 Lane Boulevard
Reno, NV 89000
September 2, 1998

Mr. Henry Lee, Director of Personnel
Asian American Museum of the West
111 West Heritage Way
Reno, NV 89000

Dear Mr. Lee:

My friend Lucyann Iwamoto suggested that I write to you regarding the position available for a computer operator in the museum's systems department. I am in the last semester of the two-year program at Reno State College and expect to receive an Associate of Arts degree in computer studies in January. Please see the enclosed résumé for more details on the summer jobs I have held that are good background for your opening.

If the position in Lucyann's department has already been filled, please let me know if you have openings in other areas for someone with my qualifications. I have worked as a clerk-typist and would be interested in an administrative position with your computer area or another department.

Please call me at the phone number on my résumé to schedule an interview or for more information about my background. Thank you.

Sincerely,
Karen Ann Tangong

APPLYING FOR A JOB AT AN ORGANIZATION YOU LIKE

Many people like to start a job search by answering classified ads for job openings and getting listings of open positions from a vocational counselor at school. As mentioned above, hearing about jobs through friends is another good avenue for your search. It is also possible to broaden your search by writing to a company or other organization that you have heard of, admire, or think would be a good place to work. In such a situation, your letter should be positive and enthusiastic, but not to the point that the person reading it will question your sincerity.

Mention a specific reason that you thought of this organization. Note, for example, "I have often heard positive reports about your company, as it is Pine Valley's largest employer." Even better, do a little research to show a real interest in the company or organization; this is usually most feasible for large employers, especially those that are nationally known or are publicly held companies. For example, you can mention something like the following: "I was impressed when I read in *Momentum* news magazine that Bubbly Cola has made major increases in sales to customers formerly loyal to the big two brands of soda pop. I hope there are some good opportunities in a company with such a bright future."

APPLYING FOR INTERNSHIPS

Many organizations today offer full-time or part-time internships to students or older workers who are making career changes. An internship can be a good opportunity to learn from experienced people in your field or a field in which you are interested. For example, you may find a position as an intern in a library or archives, in a publishing operation, or at a school.

Many, but not all, of these internships are paying positions. If you hear about an internship, write for more information. Again, you may be thinking, "Why write a letter? I could call the company and find out all about it." You want to make sure you get the right information, and asking for it in writing helps to insure your request is clear. You might reach someone on the phone as well, but that person might not have all the information you need at hand.

Here are some important questions to ask about the internship:

- What are the qualifications in terms of education and previous jobs?

- Is this a paying position, and how much does it pay?

- Will there be an opportunity to do research (writing or editing, for example), in addition to administrative duties?

- Is there any college credit available upon completion of the internship? (This is most often applicable for an internship at a university.)

- Is there a set time period for this internship (six months or one year, for example), or is it open-ended?

- Will I be asked to sign a contract?

- Who will evaluate my work as an intern, and will the evaluation be in writing?

DO I NEED A RÉSUMÉ?

Many students wonder if they need résumés when they are just starting their careers. The answer from almost all career gurus is a definite "yes." You may think that you could just fill out an application for a job and list your experience there. With so many people applying for positions today, though, your first "job" when looking for a job is to get the attention of the hiring person and get that interview (and/or the opportunity to fill out an application, if that is linked to interviewing).

Even if you are looking for an entry-level position, there is still a lot of competition from other people graduating from high school, community college, or college. Many students have had summer jobs or part-time jobs that give them relevant experience for positions they want later, and their résumés should reflect that. Many students are active in school or community activities, and those activities show initiative, social skills, and possibly other skills relevant to job-hunting.

There are various ways to organize your résumé, but none is the absolute best for everyone. For students seeking entry-level jobs, many career counselors and business writers advise leading with your education in your résumé. For more experienced job candidates, the advice is to lead with job experience, and this approach may work for students with some appropriate experience already under their belts.

SAMPLE RÉSUMÉ EMPHASIZING EDUCATION

When you think that the school you went to, or the degree or certificate you earned, is a main selling point to employers, then start with that, as in this example:

note that you do not include the word "résumé"

David Weiner
1234 Success Lane
Winnerville, OH 41900
Telephone: 506-555-1212

Education

Bachelor of Science in Business, The Ohio State University,
June 1998
   Minor: Computer science
   Honors: Ohhh My honorary society

Graduate, Winnerville High School, 1994
   Honors: President of National Honor Society

Employment

Clerk, Office of Admissions, Business School, The Ohio
State University, September 1996 through June 1998; part-
time position answering phones, entering student data on
computers, and updating mailing lists.

Waiter, Joe's Yacht Club, Upper Winnerville, Ohio,
summers of 1996, 1997; temporary position in four-star
restaurant.

Skills

Computer programming, typing 60 wpm, fluency in
German

Software experience: Word, Word Perfect, Excel, and
Power Point

References

Available upon request.

SAMPLE RÉSUMÉ EMPHASIZING JOB EXPERIENCE

When you have worked at jobs that help qualify you for a position you want, even if you are a recent graduate, start with your work history. This approach also works well for those with several years of experience.

Davida Weiner
5678 Success Way
Winnerville, OR 90000
Telephone: 719-555-1212

optional

Career objective
To obtain a graphic design position in an advertising agency that enables me to use my technical and artistic skills.

Work experience
Associate designer, Bob's Cutting Edge Agency, 1995-1996, summer 1997; used page makeup software to design print ads for two major campaigns (please see sample portfolio).

Clerk, WMPCC (World's Most Powerful Computer Company), Summer 1994; performed beta testing of new scanner, working with laser and inkjet printers.

Education
Associate of Arts, Graphic Design, Brooding Buffalo Community College, Greater Winnerville, Oregon, January 1998
>Notable courses: Archiving Images Online; Multimedia and You
>Honors: Treasurer, Ad Club

Graduate, Rogers and Clark Academy, Winnerville, OR, 1995

Community activities
Volunteer designer, monthly newsletter of the Save Our Coastline Coalition, 1997 to the present (please see sample portfolio)

References
Available upon request.

Be aware that these are by no means the only possible approaches to writing a résumé or cover letter. Job hunting is an entire field of study in itself. No doubt your school library, local library, and bookstore have countless reference books available to help you hone these skills. See "For More Information" at the end of this book for a few recommendations to get started on such a project.

FOUR

MORE BUSINESS LETTERS—GETTING THE JOB DONE

So now you have that new job you were looking for, either full-time or part-time. Often you are asked to write a letter to a customer or client, or to set up a form letter for dealing with many similar situations. The same guidelines that you used in other chapters will work well in these situations: include all needed information, be brief, and organize your material logically.

CUSTOMER SERVICE LETTERS

Every business receives complaints about products, service, or both. It is just human nature to complain, and people want to feel they are getting their money's worth when they buy something. Moreover, although customers may occasionally express themselves too angrily or seem to be annoying, the first rule for dealing with the public is still, and always will be, "The customer is always right." Whether you are a part-time clerk or the owner of a new company, you need feedback from customers; if many customers are not satisfied, the business may not survive.

When you are writing a business letter to respond to a complaint, be professional in tone, period. It does not matter if Ms. X makes sarcastic remarks suggesting that your ancestors must have crawled out from under rocks. You are responding not as an individual involved in a snappy conversation, but as a representative of an organization that would like Ms. X to spend her money on its products again in the future.

Here is a sample form letter for responding to calls or letters of complaint from individual consumers:

Tuff Toaster Company
6 Breadcrumb Road
Raisin Toast, OK 80000

March 2, 1999

Ms. Notably Angry
22 Homeowner Road
Happyville, MO 50500

Dear Ms. Angry:

Thank you for your letter (call) of (date including month, day, year). We are sorry to hear that you are unhappy with your Tuff Toaster model # _____.

Because your original warranty has expired, we can offer repair service for a fee of $20 plus parts. Send your toaster in the original carton, if possible, to the following address:

_____

Please note that the Tuff Toaster repair alcove cannot accept packages that are mailed postage due or "COD."

To keep your toaster working well in the future, we suggest that (add any special information here that you learned from the complaint—for example: You persuade your grandson not to deposit crayons in the slots where the bread goes).

Tuff Toaster wants your business and thanks you again for letting us know about this problem.

Sincerely,
Robb Rye
Customer Service Assistant

CUSTOMER SERVICE, BUSINESS TO BUSINESS

Rather than corresponding with individual consumers, as in the above example, you may need to write to another business that your organization works with. Let's say, for example, that you work for Friendly Flour Company, and the largest restaurant chain in your area (Lunch Land) is complaining about receiving its deliveries of flour late. Be specific in your reply, and explain not only what the problem is, but also what Friendly Flour is doing to fix it. For example, if delivery problems were caused by breakdowns in your fleet of trucks, explain that breakdowns were too frequent, so Friendly Flower has purchased two new trucks and changed mechanics' services for the existing fleet. The person you are writing to at Lunch Land is not interested in the details of your problems, but rather in the details of how you can provide better service in the future.

If the complaint is a serious one, and Lunch Land

is threatening to stop ordering from your company, find out if you can offer a special incentive to keep them as a customer. Ask your supervisor or whoever is the main contact with Lunch Land what the special incentive might be, and be sure to explain the incentive positively and clearly. For example, you might say, "To thank you for your patience during our recent problems with delivery, we are happy to offer you a 10 percent discount on your next order."

In any customer service letter from one business to another, make a point of including a brief statement of thanks to the other business. For example, it is good to say, "Thank you for doing business with Friendly Flour! We value you as a customer and look forward to hearing from you."

CONTESTING CHARGES ON AN INVOICE OR BILL

If you are writing to another business or professional organization to contest a charge on a bill or invoice, follow the same guidelines as above. Even if you think that the shipping department at Augie's Auto Supply is a bit sloppy about checking its invoices, be professional in tone. As with any other type of letter, put yourself in the place of the person who will read the letter you send. If you write something heated or angry about a mistake, you are less likely to get prompt service to have the error corrected. Also, your job could be in danger if the company you are writing to does not like your tone—they might turn around and complain about you.

Always be specific. Refer to an invoice or bill by its number and date (rather than "your recent invoice"). Whenever possible, enclose a copy of the invoice or bill in question. Also, enclose a copy of any other information that will help you get the mistake fixed. For example, if you have a shipping ticket dated April 3 for ten cases of 10W-30 motor oil, and a bill for twenty cases shipped the same date, be sure to enclose a copy of the shipping ticket.

When you send a letter questioning a bill your company has received, make a note on your calendar to check back with the company in thirty days (or whatever interval your supervisor recommends) if you have not received an answer.

APPOINTMENT LETTERS

Say a new dentist has set up an office in your neighborhood, and you are lucky enough to get a job in her office just as you are graduating with your two-year associate's degree in business. She asks you to set up a form letter to remind patients of their appointments. You yourself are not Gaytrice Gum, DDS, but you are representing her, so your letter must make that clear.

Office of Gaytrice Gum, DDS
32 Adult Teeth Avenue
Flossing, NJ 20000
Telephone: 012-122-5555

November 9, 1998

Mr. Fearless Patient
415 Healthy Drive
Greater Flossing, NJ 20010

Dear Mr. Patient:

This is a friendly reminder that your next appointment for a regular checkup with Dr. Gum is as follows:

Friday, December 10, 1998, 8 A.M.

This time has been reserved especially for you. As you
know, six-month checkups are the key to keeping your
mouth healthy. If you cannot keep this appointment,
please phone me at your earliest convenience.

Thank you.

Sincerely,
Benita Brace   **or "Assistant to Dr. Gum," if you**
Office of Dr. Gum ⋯⋯⋯   **want to use a title**

It is important to set special information such as the
time of the appointment in a different format to make
it more noticeable. You can center the time, as in the
example above, underline it, or put it in bold. Or you
can leave a blank line for the time and write in the appointment time neatly, if that is acceptable to your
employer.

   If you work for a school, college, or company that
offers courses or seminars to adults, you can adapt
the above letter to use as a reminder letter to students who have registered for seminars. In that situation, you may be writing from one address, such as
the school registrar's office, reminding the recipient of
an activity at another location (a student attending a
course in another building, for example). So be sure
the person has all the location information he or she
needs, and enclose directions if necessary.

A FIELD TRIP TO THE ZOO

Let's say you are a teacher's assistant or volunteer at
an elementary school and are asked to set up a trip.

The school needs permission from a parent or guardian of each child before that child can attend, and often the school collects money in advance to cover certain expenses. Every kid in the class is eager to go on the trip, and your letter can ensure that all paperwork is completed on time. Here are some pointers for this type of letter:

- Be brief and use simple language. Parents are very busy, and they are more likely to take care of the permission request if it is straight-forward.

- Emphasize the key information of the date of the trip and any money required, using under-lining, bold type, colored type, etc.

- Make it clear whether each child is expected to bring a lunch from home, bring money for lunch, or prepay for it.

- Indicate whether students need to bring addi-tional materials from home, or if the child can-not bring certain things. (The trip may be to a museum, for example, that does not allow food or beverages.)

"SEND ME A MEMO ON THAT, AJP!"

The interoffice memo (or memorandum, to use the formal word) is a basic feature of work life in many medium-sized or large offices. If you work in a small company, you may never need to write a memo. In a larger organization, though, a memo is a convenient way to summarize information for your coworkers or, more commonly, for your supervisor.

If you have a family member or friend who works in an office, he or she may wonder if writing skills are appreciated by memo readers. There is nothing wrong with the memo as a means of communication; in fact, memos are useful in many situations. But people often misuse memos by making them too long, using overblown language, or adopting a rude or unbusinesslike tone.

Here are some common reasons to write a memo to communicate at work:

- to evaluate a plan or proposal from another organization, including the pros and cons of the proposal and your own recommendations;

- to propose a new project or initiative that you would like to see adopted in your own or another department;

- to suggest changes or improvements in a policy or procedure;

- to summarize your experiences at a meeting or seminar that you attended as a representative of your organization.

These guidelines will help you write a memo that will be read and appreciated:

- Keep it factual. Answer the seven questions "who, what, when, where, how, why, and how much" as appropriate.

- Write in plain language. There's no bonus for using extra words, such as, "Relative to the project that has been discussed in detail, the Delta project. . . ." (Just say, "About the Delta project, . . . ").

- Keep the memo as brief as possible; everyone is pressed for time.

- Express yourself professionally, even in a memo you plan to mark "Confidential." For every business communication you write, it is safe to assume that a dozen people or more might read it (thus, omit any reference to "Mr. Blockhead's well-known stubbornness" or "Ms. Ramrod's ridiculous attitude toward changes"). Before you commit anything to paper, imagine that the person you're talking about will somehow read this memo and may even be your boss someday.

Before you write your first memo, ask the boss's secretary or assistant if your workplace has stipulated a format for memos. For example, some organizations ask that you start with the word "Memorandum" centered at the top of the first sheet, while others omit that. Your computer may even have a template or macro that automatically sets the format. Most commonly, you double-space the "to" and "from" information at the top but single-space between lines. The following example shows this format; also, notice how the writer responds to criticism in a smooth, professional manner:

If you have a lot of information to convey, you may want to write your memo in two parts, to ensure that it is read and understood. For example, if you are proposing that the company add a new department that will bring in revenue, don't start out writing a seven-page memo that will be too long to digest. Instead, write a two-page cover memo summarizing why Joe's Office Equipment Supermart should start a word-processing business, and then attach a business plan (which may indeed be four pages, five pages, or more) that lists details. For guidelines or suggestions on how to write a business plan, talk to the librarian in the business department of your local library.

PEOPLE'S PUBLISHING COMPANY
• *Books for you and your community* •

To: Abdul Gupta

From: Mary Smith

Date: June 19, 1998

Re: China Sea proposal

As you requested, I reviewed the response from China Sea Community Center to our outline for a book to help Asian immigrants adapt to life in the southern United States. Although there are many points of difference between us, I think we can still make this project work.

Here are some points I think we can change to compromise with China Sea:
- broaden the target audience to include southeast Asian countries, as well as the original countries of China, Japan, Korea, and India;
- include 8 to 12 photos of men, women, and children of various ages from various countries to make the point that the advice is for everyone, not just for males;
- include a section on how to use the health care system, specifically targeted to women as the mothers of children and the ones who make health care arrangements for the family.

Rather than responding to these points by letter, however, I think we should propose a meeting between several of us from People's Publishing and the board of China Sea. That way, we can discuss in an atmosphere of good will what kinds of changes would make their board more comfortable with the book and even—we hope—eager to participate.

I hope that we can meet next week. Please let me know what day and time you prefer. Also, I would be happy to invite the China Sea leadership; let me know if you would prefer to do that from your office. Thank you.

For another example, you may be working as an editorial assistant at a publishing company and want to propose a new book on a favorite topic of yours. Rather than writing five or six pages to explain your idea, try composing a one-page cover memo suggesting the title, such as *Promoting Your Band or Other Music Act,* and mentioning the highlights of the book and the possible market. Then you can add an outline of several pages to develop your idea in detail, including types of promotion (press releases about forthcoming appearances of a band, advertising your compact disc in local newspapers, or distributing demonstration cassettes to radio stations). The cover memo should tempt the reader to want to know more about your idea.

FAX MANIA

Many people today send letters via fax. The word fax is a commonly used abbreviation for the term telefacsimile. The fax itself is a machine that is capable of scanning documents and transmitting, receiving, and printing them. You may choose to send a formal letter, nicely word-processed as usual on your organization's letterhead, via fax with or without a cover sheet. Or you may write or type a few lines on a fax cover sheet and just transmit that.

Faxes are an excellent way to introduce yourself to someone who is difficult to reach by phone. They also prove useful for transmitting detailed information. For example, you receive a phone message asking for the names of three contacts in your sales department; rather than spelling out the names in another phone message and listing their phone extensions, you can quickly and neatly fax the information.

Many organizations instruct you to fax a letter so that the recipient will get it immediately and then mail

Tuff Toaster Company
Raisin Toast, OK 80000
Fax number: 808-555-1211

FAX

To: [name]
_____

[company]
_____

[their fax number]
_____

From: [your name]
_____

[your department or title]
_____

[your phone number]
_____

Message:

[leave a blank space of several inches here for typing, or add ruled lines if you will be writing messages by hand]

Total pages including this sheet: _____

If you have problems reading any of the pages in this transmission, please phone Wanda Wheat at 1-800-637-1412.

the original letter to the same person. If you do this, stamp the letter or write neatly at the top, "sent via fax [date]." This will prevent the recipient from being confused about receiving two copies. Other organizations now choose not to mail the letter after they have faxed it. Ask what the policy is in your workplace.

You may be asked to set up a fax cover sheet, particularly if you are working for a new business or setting up a business yourself. Make sure to include your fax number in return and also a phone number the recipient can call in case there are any transmission problems, that is, difficulty reading the fax. Also important is a line or box for you to mark how many sheets you are faxing; this way the recipient knows if he or she has all the pages needed. A sample fax cover sheet incorporating all the points you need appears on page 69.

FIVE

ℰLECTRONIC MAIL

In many ways, "e-mail" has changed the way people think about letters. You write a conventional letter ("snail mail" to e-mail enthusiasts) in a certain format, copy it for your files, mail it, and then wait for the recipient to receive it and open it. Even if you are in a hurry, the person may not get your letter for a couple of days. And it is probably smart, given the variables of mail service, to assume that it will take a week for someone to get your letter and open it. By contrast, using e-mail, you can send a message quickly—in minutes or seconds—across town, to another state, or another country. All you need is a computer with a modem, a device that attaches to a telephone line or some other communication path, and an e-mail software program.

In many ways, e-mail is similar to any business mail: Your best approach is to express yourself simply, briefly, and very clearly. As we have seen, the business letter in general needs to be brief or at least concise—that is, expressing all the necessary thoughts in the smallest number of words and sentences. This is even more true for an e-mail than for a business letter. Why? Time is at a premium online. For one thing, the recipient may pay a monthly fee to a company that provides the host computer (which allows you to connect to the Internet) and a monthly telephone bill for charges incurred while hooked up to "the Net." In that situation, time truly is money.

But aside from the financial factor, everyone is busy today. Even if your e-mail correspondent is writing from his or her workplace, and so does not have to pay for the privilege of using e-mail, that person is sure to be busy. He or she is working on other documents and/or e-mailing other people in and out of the workplace; your e-mail may be read while your correspondent is trying to complete an urgent project on another screen.

PARTS OF AN E-MAIL MESSAGE

To enjoy the convenience of sending and receiving e-mail, you need to master the first step of addressing your message. If you are using e-mail at your workplace, and there is an in-house computer network for reaching your colleagues and supervisors, follow the instructions for that system to type in the name or, often, to star it in an "address book" (often called a nickname list) or in-house list of personnel.

To access someone out in the world (that is, not in your workplace in an internal directory), generally you start by accessing the "to" space or window and typing in the following:

joe@companyname.org

The two basic parts of the address are the mailbox on the destination computer ("joe") and the host part following the "at" symbol ("companyname.org), which identifies the Internet service provider.

Remember that the computer is "dumb" in the sense that it cannot guess what you meant to type into it. If you are off by one letter or one punctuation mark, the message will not go through. Note especially in the preceding example that there are no spaces between any of the elements of the address; even "companyname" is run together. If you have located the name "Rap Recording Hood," that name as part of an e-mail address must be typed as "raprecordinghood."

Some e-mail addresses may include an underline; again using the example above, substitute "joe_player@companyname.org." Any punctuation, just like regular characters, must be included as shown. If you misread the underline and use a hyphen instead, the message will not go through. So it's worth a brief amount of your time to double-check the address and proofread it on your screen before you send the message, especially if this is the first time you've written to the person.

If you are just starting to use e-mail, friends will give you their e-mail addresses. Where else do you get e-mail addresses for those you want to write to? Ask your school librarian or town librarian if the library has a hard-copy directory of e-mail addresses. Many newspapers and magazines now have pages or sections of interesting computer sites that include their addresses; if you see, for example, a listing of sites or newsgroups (usenet groups) for people who love horses, you can clip and save the article for future reference. Most search engines have online directories that you can access, but some charge a fee.

Other parts of an e-mail message, in addition to the address, are as follows:

- Message title—This may be called "subject," "re," or "topic" on your particular system.

Friends, especially students, often write very casual and/or supposedly humorous titles for their messages, such as "duh" or "huh" or "WHAT girl?" For business messages, however, it is good to use a straightforward descriptive title, and it helps the recipient if you don't use the same title each time. Instead of heading every message "Fox Network project," for example, use "Deadline for Fox Network project" on one, "Financial question re Fox" on another, and "Edits on Fox Network project" on another message. That way, if someone is storing your messages online to access later, he or she does not need to open every message of a dozen or more pertaining to the same project (and that same convenience will be available to you).

• Body of the message—This is usually called "message," "text," or "your words" on your system. This is the essence of your message, what you want to say and get across; see "Content of your message" below for more details on what to include.

• Lists for "cc" and "bcc"—Addresses for those to whom you want to send "carbon copies" or "blind carbon copies" are included here. On some systems, to send an e-mail to someone outside your home or workplace, you must repeat the person's address under "cc" or "bcc"; follow the instructions that come with your e-mail server. When sending e-mails at work, don't get into the habit of sending a "cc" of each message to your boss's boss. Think about the interests of the main recipient before cc-ing others; if the message contains confidential information just for the recipient, he or she will not want you to show that message to others.

- Attached computer file—This is one of the greatest conveniences of e-mail. You can send a document with your message for review by the recipient. For example, let's say you work for the county parks' department and are on the committee to increase recycling in each park. You have drafted a quick list of your suggestions, as you had a lot of ideas to share. Rather than printing and copying one document to distribute to the committee via interoffice mail or US mail, you can simply write a brief e-mail to each person on the committee and attach the document with your list of recycling ideas. See below for additional tips on forwarding your résumé via e-mail to apply for a job.

CONTENT OF YOUR MESSAGE

One of the most important e-mail tips is that each message should stand alone. That is, to understand and answer your message, the person receiving it should not have to access other messages from you or to you. Here's a simple example: You are in purchasing and send an e-mail to Letitia Jones in communications. You ask her if she wants red report covers or silver report covers for her new proposal. You are out of the office for several days and return to find a reply from Letitia that says, "Yes, the first one." So you have to go back to your own message and then send her another one saying, "By that do you mean red?" By this time, she might not remember the original question!

In some e-mail systems, you can attach the message you received to your reply, so remember to do that if it helps make your message clear. If you do not have that convenience on your e-mail, then you would want her to reply like this, "Silver report covers are good; the quantity is 250, yes?" This way you have confirmation of the color, plus, a useful reminder of the quantity, too.

Sometimes it is necessary to refer to another e-mail already on file. Perhaps the original message was a detailed budget or schedule that is too long and involved to retype. In such cases, you can refer to "my message Fox budget, April 23" and ask the person if he or she still has that on file. If not, you can resend or print out the April 23 message. On some systems, you can forward your old message or re-send. As you use any particular e-mail server, you will pick up other tips for saving time and sending messages more efficiently.

As important as it is to be concise in a conventional business letter, it is twice as important when writing e-mail. Sometimes students think it sounds businesslike or dignified to throw in a lot of long words or windy phrases; this is always boring and especially useless in e-mail.

How do you sign an e-mail message? You will naturally notice that your e-mail server has included your name in the "from" box or window. Most people still sign the text with their name or initials. That's not always enough, however. In many business messages, particularly the first or second time you are writing to someone online, it's advisable to include your full name, title, and telephone number; this helps the person place you and helps him or her reply. Also, if he or she needs to forward your message to someone else, that person will then also know who you are and how to get in touch with you.

This sample message incorporates a lot of the above information:

To: joe@companyname.com
cc: maria@companyname.com

From: jane@parkdistrict.org

Re: Meeting of the park district board

Message:
Hi Joe and Maria: Because you are the president and secretary of the board, please let me know if this time will work for the next board meeting—Tuesday, January 17, at 4 p.m.

Also, I've attached a draft agenda for the meeting. Please review and let me know if you want to add items or change the order of the agenda.—Thanks, Jane Electronic-Woman, Administrative Assistant, Friendlyville Park District, 630-555-1212

Sent: January 2, 1998, 9 a.m.

Attachment: WPfile: agenda1

APPLYING FOR JOBS VIA E-MAIL—YOUR RÉSUMÉ SPEEDS THROUGH CYBERSPACE

Many help-wanted classified ads are still written as they have been for years, directing any interested applicants to mail their résumés to the company or organization, or to mail the résumés to a box number at the newspaper where the ad is running. There are at least a couple of circumstances, however, in which you can send your résumé via e-mail. One is when you have located a job opening on an organization's home page on the web; normally, the list of positions open includes a brief list of qualifications needed and ends with the e-mail address for the recruiter responsible for screening candidates. In this case, your "cover letter" via e-mail is a message saying that you saw the listing for the position and want to apply for that job; you can send your résumé at the same time as an attached file. The classified ads in the newspaper, most often those for computer jobs, might simply ask you to reply or forward your résumé to an e-mail address.

If you are specifically interested in finding a job via the Internet, try accessing the following site, Monsterboard, which compiles and displays information from many sources on various types of occupations in various locations. You can reach Monsterboard at

http://www.monster.com/

When sending out your résumé to a variety of organizations, possibly around the country or around the world, you have no way of knowing which word-processing system is used at the receiving organization. It is useful, therefore, in the word-processing program that you use, to convert your résumé to a "text file," which can then be read by any word-processing program and converted to its format. That way, the organization to which you are applying does not have to spend time trying to figure out how to access or print the résumé you want everyone to read and appreciate.

CONFIDENTIALITY OF E-MAIL

Some children play with imaginary friends, or believe in ghosts and other imaginary beings. Confidentiality of e-mail at work is virtually imaginary, too. Oprah Winfrey and her guest Carol Kleiman, career and jobs writer for the *Chicago Tribune*, said it best on a program segment in early 1997 devoted to e-mail: "Just picture any message you send," advised Kleiman, "as printed on the front page of the *Tribune* or another newspaper."

Every company or organization that operates an e-mail system keeps the messages you send and receive, even after they are deleted. Those messages can be subpoenaed in court in lawsuits involving a variety of issues, such as equal opportunity employment or sexual harrassment. You can be putting your job, and/or your organization, at risk for various legal complications with a hasty or supposedly humorous line here or there.

Also, most organizations offer supervisors the opportunity to scan their employees' messages, and you would not be notified that your mail is screened in this way. So, though e-mail is convenient, accessible, and fun, resist the temptation to type, "Old Mr. Rigidity doesn't do much all day for his $150,000 a year, does he?" If Mr. Rigidity sees that message, he might just fire you.

There are a number of ways Mr. Rigidity can see the message; he does not even have to look into your directory or that of your e-mail recipient. Someone can print out the message, thinking it's something fun to mail to a friend who used to work with you.

When you send a job to print on a computer, the printer may jam—and often it seems that it is most likely to jam if there's a confidential or sensitive document being printed. Then, if someone else comes along to clear the jammed printer, he or she is likely to see your e-mail—it might be Mr. Rigidity himself. Or your friendly coworker may forward your message to a third party, who forwards it to someone else, say, Mr. Rigidity's assistant.

Flirting online is common in organizations that use e-mail to link their employees together. Again, picture the message you want to send on the front page of a newspaper or on your boss's desk. For any subject matter, in fact, use common sense. Do not use company e-mail for explicit sexual messages. Do not carry on emotionally intense dialogues regarding a relationship on your work e-mail system. You sometimes get a deliciously private feeling when you receive a complimentary e-mail or a very friendly invitation from someone. Beware, however, that it is a deceptive feeling because there is no privacy online. Most people who have e-mail at work do occasionally use it to arrange lunch appointments, or may throw in an occasionally catty comment on Keisha's new lime green and purple shirt. That's fine, but to act responsibly (and to keep your job), keep all nonbusiness communications under control.

INTERNET SAFETY IN "CHAT ROOMS"

Many Net users, young and old, participate in a chat area or chat room: an area devoted to typed "real time" conversations with other individuals who share an interest. There are many chat rooms for fans of various types of literature, including science fiction, murder mysteries, and poetry. Many other chat rooms are health oriented; those with a specific disease or condition, or who have a family member with this condition, write back and forth to exchange information and offer support.

Sex on the Internet is a highly controversial and complex topic. If you are a young person corresponding via the Internet with people whom you have never met, you need to observe a few common-sense rules to protect yourself. Be wary of someone who claims to be your age, if you are thirteen or fourteen, for example, but who has a very adult vocabulary and adult interests. Be especially careful if you have a joined a sci-fi chat room, for example, but someone keeps writing to you only about sex. Use your first name only in your messages, and do not give out your phone number or address to strangers.

In recent years, a number of young people have been sexually assaulted by adults posing as teenagers who asked to meet them away from home. Your best bet is not to arrange a personal meeting outside your home with an e-mail correspondent. But if you do decide to meet him or her, make sure you tell someone you trust where you are going and the name and e-mail address of the person you are meeting. The meeting should occur in a public place, such as a mall, and you should have a friend or parent accompany you. All this may help you get home safely.

MANNERS ONLINE

Even though the Internet is relatively new, some definite etiquette is already agreed upon by Net users as a group. First of all, do not type your messages in all capital letters; that's called *shouting* and is considered rude and aggressive.

It is also important to avoid *flaming*, which is insulting someone online or intruding aggressively as a newcomer to a computer chat group. Every chat room is a group of like-minded individuals or people with very similar concerns. Yes, you have a constitutional right to express yourself and your views, but to just charge in and try to aggressively impose your views is considered bad manners on the Internet. If you persist in posting negative messages when you are asked to stop, someone in the group may send a message to the Internet service provider asking that you be blocked from sending messages to the chat room group.

Spamming is the sending of your message—or especially your advertisement or marketing materials—to huge numbers of users, whether it might be of interest to them or not. Many Internet users post their messages to huge mailing lists or chat groups, without regard for the nature of the group, and most people do not want to receive "junk e-mail," just as they are not fond of junk mail.

The Internet offers a wealth of information to those doing research and a great field of opportunity for those who want to correspond via e-mail. Common sense and some manners will help you make the greatest use of the Net's potential.

SIX

WRITE IT RIGHT: GRAMMAR AND WORD USAGE

The word "grammar" often has a paralyzing effect on students, and this has been true for generations. Do not imagine that your grandparents loved to study grammar—unless they were writers or English teachers. But there is no reason to be afraid of grammar, which is the study of words and how they fit together, especially in sentences.

Your best approach is to think of grammar as an aide to helping you express yourself better. You have a lot of great ideas to put across in your community group, you want to get that special job at the Nature Conservancy, or you want to get a scholarship to study music in Asia. To achieve one or more of these goals, you need to write a good letter, craft a fine résumé, and compose a statement about your qualifications that will convince people to give you what you want. Writing clearly and effectively will help you reach these goals.

Many good books have been published to help you deal with questions about grammar, spelling, and word usage, including *How to Improve Your Grammar and Usage* in the Speak Out, Write On! series. Other books are listed in "For More Information" at the end of this book. If you can buy one or two of these books, that's great. Otherwise, locate them at your school library or public library.

TYPES OF SENTENCES

A *sentence* is usually defined as a complete thought. Here are some examples:

The dinosaur chased Ooogie through the valley.

Skydiving can be dangerous.

I am so happy that I feel like dancing.

Aliens do not live next door to you.

Each sentence has a subject (a noun or pronoun—for example, "dinosaur" in the first sentence above) and a predicate (a verb or verb-adverb combination—for example, "chased" in the first sentence above). Parts of speech, such as the noun and the verb, will be discussed below.

A phrase and a clause are also parts of sentences. A *phrase* is a group of words that modify, or describe, something. Example: *Born on a ranch* [phrase], Maria always loved horses. A clause is a group of words with a separate thought that does not stand alone as a sentence. Example: Sam accepted the job, *although he did not know if he would like the work* [clause].

Here are the three main types of sentences:

Simple sentence: Jose walked to the games arcade.

Compound sentence, which combines two thoughts in separate clauses: Jose walked to the games arcade, and he met Moses at three o'clock.

84

Complex sentence, which adds a qualifying clause to a basic sentence: Jose walked to the games arcade, even though it is three miles from his house.

In a business letter, memo, or any other type of business writing, it is best to write in complete sentences. An employer wants to know that you can write correctly, and this is true even if you want to be a computer operator or an electrician. You still have to write memos and reports as a computer operator or in other technical jobs.

In personal correspondence you may occasionally use a sentence *fragment*. This is a collection of words that is not a complete sentence by itself. Often an expression we use in everyday conversation is easily understood but does not constitute a sentence. For example, you might write or say "no problem" to a friend who asks a favor; your meaning is clear, but the words "no problem" do not make up a full sentence. You might say to a brother or sister, "What a nut!" This is a sentence fragment, almost a kind of shorthand for a complete sentence, which would be "What a nut you are!" As long as your meaning is clear, there is no problem using sentence fragments in personal writing.

Clear and simple writing wins the day most of the time. Don't pile a lot of useless ten-dollar words onto your sentence, as someone would pile furniture onto a pickup truck, because the sentence might be too overloaded to do its job! There's no prize for using long words or writing the longest sentence.

QUICK REVIEW OF PARTS OF SPEECH

We classify words as parts of speech to help determine how to use them best.

Noun

A person or thing. Examples: boy, girl, dog, computer, Freddie, Linda, White House.

As mentioned above, a noun is usually the subject of a sentence—the actor or the doer.

Pronoun

A shorthand way of referring to a person or thing. Examples: it, you, me, they.

Verb

An action word or a word that describes a condition. Examples: walk, run, scream, challenge, defy, is, are. As mentioned earlier, a verb or verb phrase ("is running") is the predicate of a sentence.

Adverb

A word that describes a verb. Examples: quickly, slowly, fast, deeply, loudly. Adverbs often end in "-ly," but not always.

Adjective

A word that describes a noun. Examples: blue, red, big, beautiful, hideous, thoughtful, brilliant. Beginning writers often use too many adjectives. Especially in letters, be careful not to overuse adjectives as a sign of your enthusiasm. That just looks like sloppy writing.

Preposition

A word that ties together a phrase with a noun or pronoun. Examples: in, into, on, above, over.

Conjunction

A word that links two clauses or phrases. Examples: and, but, or.

"WHAT IS THEY?"

Subject-verb agreement is another aspect of writing that sounds harder than it really is. Most readers have noticed the mistake in the subhead above. To be correct, the subhead should ask, "What are they?" The big question in subject-verb agreement usually comes down to this: Should the verb have an "s" on the end? Or, if the verb is a form of "to be," should it be "is" or "are"?

A plural subject normally takes a verb without the "s." For example, it is correct to say, "Rita and Latoya walk to the river." For a singular subject, we need the "s." For example, "Latoya walks to the river."

Again, if you have difficulty telling which form of the verb goes with the noun, it is best to consult a handbook of grammar, style, or writing. See "For More Information" later in this book.

GO, WENT, GONE

Verb tenses are easy to master, if you just take some time to think about it. Present tense is used to describe something happening now. Example: "I *work* at Joe's Tacqueria every week." Past tense describes something that is complete or finished. Example: "I *worked* at Joe's Tacqueria for six months, until they noticed that I was eating up all the profits." Past perfect tense is used to talk about something that was completed before something else. Example: "I *had worked* at the bank before I worked at Joe's." Present perfect tense describes something that started in the past but may still occur again in the future. Example, "I *have worked* at Joe's Tacqueria from time to time."

In the English language, many regular verbs change from past to present by adding a "d" or "ed."

Examples: talk/talked, walk/walked, move/moved, climb/climbed. For many irregular verbs, however, you need to memorize the past and past perfect tenses, as they are not so predictable. Some examples: go/went/have gone, do/did/have done, sing/sang/have sung.

Sometimes the verb in English depends on whether the noun or pronoun you are using with the verb is first person ("I" or "we), second person ("you," singular or plural), or third person ("he," "she," or "they"). Some of the most commonly used verbs are various forms of the infinitive "to be." Correct forms are "I am" for first person, "you are" for second person, and "she is" for third person. If you are still learning English, write down some of these common exceptions to the rules in a reminder list for yourself.

SPELLING

Now you're confident you have mastered sentences and parts of speech. How's your spelling? A misspelled word can stick out like a sore thumb. Think about your cover letter and résumé when you are applying for jobs: one misspelled word is often enough to deny you an interview. So it's worth your while to make sure every word is spelled correctly.

If you are writing on a computer, use a spell-checking program, if you have one. A spell-checking program commonly gives you alternatives to a word it identifies as spelled incorrectly. You must then approve the proper substitution. You still need to proofread your own work carefully, too, to make sure that you have not overlooked a problem. Be careful of homonyms (words that sound alike but that are different in meaning)—the spell-checking program will not alert you to the use of *hear* when you mean *here*.

Even with a spell-checking feature on a computer,

you need a good dictionary to verify definitions of words as well as the appropriate spelling. *Webster's New Collegiate Dictionary* or *American Heritage Dictionary* are popular choices among teachers and students.

WORD USAGE

Whether you are a beginning writer or an experienced one, you want to target your writing to your intended audience. If you are applying for a job or writing a letter to the editor of the *New York Times*, you probably should not use slang expressions such as "way excellent" or "then I go" (for "then I said"). Slang is fine in personal letters to friends and in e-mail that is not strictly business.

Be straightforward in your word choices. Do not refer to yourself in the third person, as former Senator Robert Dole often did in his unsuccessful campaign for the US presidency in 1996. (He frequently said, "Bob Dole thinks. . . .") This is confusing and pretentious, especially for students or young people.

Connotation is the meaning attached to words other than the straight dictionary definition. Consider the difference between "Hung Wha pondered the choices too long" and "Hung Wha considered his options carefully." Try to be nonemotional in your business letters, even if you are writing a letter of complaint about a product or service or if you are writing a letter to the editor with your political views. You might feel better momentarily if you write a letter that uses words as arrows to attack someone, but realistically, what are your chances of convincing the uncommitted when you write in that manner?

Use technical jargon sparingly in a letter or résumé. It may be that the first person screening your job application is a personnel recruiter or a personnel clerk. Even if you are applying for a job as a computer programmer or engineer, you need to communicate clearly with people who may not know technical terms. Your letter should be professional and should not depend on technical terms to get your points across.

Similarly, do not load your business correspondence with initials abbreviating terms or acronyms for names of organizations and so on. You may appear pompous if you give the impression you do not have the time to spell out a name or term. For example, do not use "ASAP" (as soon as possible) except in very informal notes or e-mails. Also, the acronym you may be familiar with may stand for something else to your listener; is "ADA" short for American Dental Association, American Dietetic Association, or Assistant District Attorney?

It is to your credit as a well-read person if you can quote from some of the classics of literature. Many people find themselves quoting, "To be or not to be," the famous line from Shakespeare's *Hamlet*, at one time or another. But basically you should reserve all literary quotations and flowery phrases for your creative writing, including poetry, or for your personal letters. Again, keeping your business letters straightforward is always a good goal.

At the same time, writing in a businesslike manner does not mean you have to be dull. I admit I was immediately captivated by a cover letter with a résumé from a prospective editorial assistant that began, "When I read the ad for your position, I was amazed at how closely I fit the qualifications you are looking for." This fresh, enthusiastic approach appealed to me, and I called to offer an appointment for a job interview.

SEVEN

SOURCES TO USE AT THE LIBRARY

For many letters that you write, you may already have all the information you need at your fingertips. If you are answering a "help wanted" classified ad in the newspaper, the ad will tell you where to send your letter. But for other letters, you will need to locate or develop information. Let's say you have always wanted to work at Compact Disc Corporate Paradise, but you don't have the address; also, you would like to do a little research to include some impressive fact about the company in your cover letter. You should certainly try to find the information you need for your letter at the library or on the World Wide Web.

To take another example, suppose you are secretary of your school's student council, and the council wants to involve other schools and some community groups in a recycling campaign. You may have the names of all the groups you want to write to, but not the addresses or the ZIP codes. It is vital to include postal ZIP codes on all your mail to help achieve timely delivery.

BASIC REFERENCE BOOKS

For almost any type of writing, you need to refer regularly to a dictionary to check spellings and to verify that you are using the word you want (not a homonym). Also, you should have handy, or know where to find at the library, a *thesaurus*, a reference book that offers synonyms—words similar in meaning to the one you have in mind. If you are writing a paper about Rodin's sculpture, "The Thinkers," you may notice you have used the word "thoughtful" five or six times. You could then look in a thesaurus to find other words to use, for example, "pensive" or "reflective."

A general encyclopedia is the best source to look up facts on a variety of topics. Authoritative and popular encyclopedias in most school or town libraries include *Grolier's Multimedia Encyclopedia*, *Compton's Encyclopedia* on CD-ROM, *Encyclopedia Americana*, *Encyclopaedia Britannica*, and *World Book*. You may need to look up "manatee" in an encyclopedia to find out more specific information about that animal before you write a letter to your US Senator on saving the manatee; the television show that got you interested in this topic may not have been very specific, or you may not have had time to write down the information you heard.

No doubt you've been told that it is not acceptable to use an encyclopedia as your only source (or even the main source) for a research paper. But encyclopedias include many useful facts that will help you understand more about nature, science, sports, history, geography, literature, and other subjects. Encyclopedias are also useful for job searches, because you may need to look up an unfamiliar term you see in an ad, and you'll want more background than you can find in a dictionary.

Dictionaries of quotations are useful for many types of writing, and these are also found in the general reference section of your library. *Bartlett's Familiar Quotations* is probably the most famous book of quotations, but many other books of quotations are now available. These include books of famous or notable sayings by women, African-Americans, business leaders, and so on.

Another good general reference source for all of your writing, including letters, is the *Reader's Guide to Periodical Literature*. This is an index published annually, with frequent updates during the year, of articles in general interest magazines such as *Time, Newsweek, US News and World Report, Smithsonian*, and the *New York Times Magazine*. You can look up possible subject headings, including the names of famous individuals or corporations, to locate articles about them.

Also in the general reference section or department of your library is a very handy directory, the *Encyclopedia of Associations*. This multi-volume reference book, updated annually, lists names, addresses, phone numbers, key contacts, and other useful information on associations and voluntary groups (as opposed to for-profit companies). Here you can access such information as the headquarters address and phone number for the March of Dimes or the American Bar Association. Or you can find answers to such questions as, "Is there a society for both stamp collecting and coin collecting?" (there is) and figure out how to get in touch with that group.

BUSINESS RESEARCH

It is very useful to get to know the business section of your library, whether you are starting a job search, changing jobs, or working in a job that involves sending out correspondence. A good basic source for information about corporations is *Standard & Poor's Register of Corporations, Directors, and Executives*, published each year by the Standard & Poor Corporation. (The name varies a little with the annual editions, but just make sure the book you are looking at is a Standard & Poor's directory.) This reference book includes the full name and address of the headquarters of corporations, useful information about their lines of business, and names and titles of key executives. Why do you need these names and titles? It is always best when applying for a job "cold"—that is, with no classified ad or recommendation—to address your letter to a specific person at the company; this improves the chances of having your letter read and answered.

The largest corporations in the United States are described in *Standard & Poor's 500 Guide*, published annually. This reference volume includes information on the five hundred largest and most successful corporations, by dollar volume of business. You may need to consult this book, for example, if you are looking for major corporations to support a campaign for healthier babies in the southern United States. There's no sense directing your appeals to the Struggling Guys and a Girlfriend Company down the street if they do not have a large operating budget for their new business; you need companies with major resources.

The business section of your library is also a good place to look if you are interested in material about careers. Often a school or town library has a career section or career corner within it, including vertical files of information about careers filed alphabetically by the name of the career. For example, under "G" for "geologist," you might find pamphlets from the American Association for the Advancement of Science and the American Petroleum Institute on this career.

Basic information on careers is published by the US government. Consult the *Occupational Outlook Handbook*, published every one or two years by the US Department of Labor, Bureau of Labor Statistics, for information on what a geologist does, what education you need to prepare for this job, and the projected future demand for people trained in this career.

Updated information about careers is available in the *Occupational Outlook Quarterly*, a periodical published every three months by the US Department of Labor. This periodical contains interesting articles on changes in demand for various careers, as well as facts about new careers arising in fast-changing areas such as health care or computer science. As this book was being prepared, "webmaster" was a new occupation being developed at many companies that have home pages on the Internet, to maintain and update those home pages, and handle e-mail from around the world. As the Internet is a new field, you would expect to find information about it in the *Quarterly* rather than in a book that may have been prepared two or three years before its publication date.

Your library may have a copy of *America's Top 300 Jobs*, a book published by JIST Works from data compiled for the Occupational Outlook Handbook. The advantage of using selected information from the handbook is that it may be more useful and interesting to you than some of the little-known careers for which there is a very small or decreasing demand today.

Books about how to write a résumé are often included in the business library. Check your card catalog or online catalog to see which titles are available. Many sources on the Internet—especially writing centers maintained by college or university English departments—also give valuable advice on how to write a résumé and in particular how to send one via e-mail.

ZIP CODE DIRECTORIES

If you need just one or two ZIP codes for your letters, it may be easiest to phone the US Postal Service to get that information. Generally, however, it is difficult to get through on the phone lines. Also, it is impractical to phone if you need to look up a list of numbers—for example, if you are doing a good-sized mailing to start a job search, or if you need to write to a number of other companies or groups to organize a project at work.

A basic reference book in most libraries and post offices is the *National Zip Code Directory*, published each year by the US Postal Service. Be sure to look for the most recent volume available. Also widely available is the *National Directory of Post Offices with ZIP Codes*, published in Columbia, Maryland, by a US Postal Service licensee.

If the computer you use is equipped with a CD-ROM drive, you can access ZIP codes on the *Microsoft Bookshelf*. This is an electronic library consisting of several disks, one of which includes a national five-digit ZIP code directory. If you or your family purchased a home computer, check to see if there is a ZIP code directory included in the software or CD-ROM diskettes that came with your system. Finally, the Internet has readily-available sources for address information, such as the "ZIP+4 Code Lookup."

ADDITIONAL RESOURCES

With the information in this book, and help from sources at your library as indicated in this chapter, you will be well equipped to write letters for any purpose, whether business or personal. If you plan to write a letter to a person with a special title (the Pope or the President of the United States), please see "Special Titles and Salutations" in the appendix at the back of this book. For further reading on the topics of letters, résumés, or business correspondence, please see "For More Information" in the back of this book. As always, if you have any further questions, your teacher or your librarian are the best people to ask first. Good luck with all that you write!

EIGHT

FAMOUS WRITERS, FAMOUS LETTERS

Throughout this book, we focus on letters as a useful means of communication in your daily life. Letters are also, however, a versatile and beautiful means of communication in the hands of some writers. Many letters are remembered because they are works of literature in themselves, because they express notable thoughts of famous people, or because they discuss important events or time periods in history. The letters in this chapter were chosen to help stimulate your thought processes and make you aware of letters as good writing.

FAMOUS PEOPLE, NOTABLE EVENTS

These letters offer interesting or quotable thoughts from famous people, or people in public life. Whether you have heard of these people or not, whether they lived recently or a long time ago, their words have something to say to today's readers.

Jonathan Swift

Author of the famous satire *Gulliver's Travels*, Swift is always remembered for his biting sense of humor, which he turns on himself in this excerpt:

Letter to Miss Vanbromrigh, August 1720:
"If Heaven had looked upon riches to be a valuable thing, it would not have given them to such a scoundrel."

Benjamin Franklin

The noted political figure, inventor, and writer was a key player in the American Revolution. Here are famous quotations from two of his letters:

Letter to Josiah Quincy, September 1773: "There never was a good war or a bad peace."

Letter to M. Leroy, 1789: "Our Constitution is in actual operation; everything appears to promise that it will last; but in this world nothing is certain but death and taxes."

Helen Maria Williams

Letters have long been important in politics and government, and sometimes the writing of letters has been a key part of revolutions. English writer Helen Williams lived in France during the French Revolution in the late eighteenth century. At first, she enthusiastically supported the French Revolution in her letters home to England. But then, as the revolutionary committee imprisoned and executed more and more people with guillotines—in the so-called Reign of Terror—Williams herself began to be suspected of treason, and her letters put her life in danger:

I had written to my friends in England, a few letters about the period of the Terror, and unfortunately, someone had the imprudence to insert extracts from them in the London journals. This indiscretion compromised my status in the eyes of the Committee of Public Safety, and this awful band began to direct its attention to me. . . . Thus I passed the winter at Paris, with the knife of the guillotine suspended over me by a frail thread.

Fortunately, Williams was not executed. She continued to write letters to England and to smuggle out of France letters from prisoners and from people trying to stop the Reign of Terror. For a time, she was exiled in Switzerland, where she still tried to help the French legislators fighting the Terror. How did the Committee on Public Safety try to stop the legislators?

The barriers of the city were shut, all communication cut off, the secrecy of letters violated, the hall of the convention blockaded by an armed force.

Jose Maria Morelos

Letters played a key role in the birth of the country of Mexico. The first president of Mexico and two of his aides wrote the following earnest and eloquent letter to US President James Madison in July 1815. Mexico had recently declared its independence from Spain and asked for support from the United States:

Puruaran, Mexico, July 14, 1815

To: James Madison, President of the United States

Most Excellent Sir:

The Mexican people, weary of the enormous weight of Spanish domination and having forever lost the

hope of being happy under the rule of their con-
querors, broke through the barriers of moderation and,
facing difficulties and perils which seemed insupera-
ble to the efforts of an enslaved colony, they raised the
cry of freedom and heavily undertook the work of re-
generation.

We relied on the protection of Heaven which could
not withdraw it from the well-known justice of our
cause nor ignore the rectitude and purity of our inten-
tions exclusively bent on the good of mankind: we relied on the mettle and enthusiasm of our compatriots,
who had decided to die rather than to again bear the
shameful yoke of slavery: and finally we relied on the
powerful aid of the United States, which as they
widely guided us by their example would favor us
with their generous assistance upon signing treaties of
friendship and alliance in which good faith would pre-
side and where the reciprocal interests of both nations
would be remembered. . . .

Jose Maria Morelos, President of Mexico
Jose Maria Linaga
Remigio de Yarza, Secretary of Government

Frederick Douglass

Born a slave, Frederick Douglass ran away from his
"master" and became a writer and leader of the antislavery movement. In 1848, he wrote this very powerful letter to Thomas Auld, his former owner, on the
occasion of the tenth anniversary of his freedom.
Although the letter was addressed to Auld, Douglass
wrote it for publication in antislavery literature and in
general newspapers. This letter explains in very
human terms why one man or woman cannot and
should not own another:

September 1848

Thomas Auld:

Sir—The long and intimate, though by no means friendly relation which unhappily subsisted between you and myself, leads me to hope that you will easily account for the great liberty which I now take in addressing you in this open and public manner. The same fact may possibly remove any disagreeable surprise which you may experience on again finding your name coupled with mine, in any other way than in an advertisement, accurately describing my person, and offering a large sum for my arrest. . . .

I have selected this day on which to address you, because it is the anniversary of my emancipation; and knowing of no better way, I am led to this as the best mode of celebrating that truly important event. Just ten years ago this beautiful September morning, yon bright sun beheld me a slave—a poor, degraded chattel— trembling at the sound of your voice, lamenting that I was a man, and wishing myself a brute. The hopes which I had treasured up for weeks of a safe and successful escape from your grasp, were powerfully confronted at this last hour by dark clouds of doubt and fear, making my person shake and my bosom to heave with the heavy contest between hope and fear. I have no words to describe to you the deep agony of soul which I experienced on that never to be forgotten morning— (for I left by daylight). I was making a leap in the dark. The probabilities, so far as I could by reason determine them, were stoutly against the undertaking. . . . One in whom I had confided, and who had promised me assistance, appalled by fear at the trial hour, deserted me, thus leaving the responsibility of success or failure solely with myself. . . .

When yet but a child about six years old, I imbibed the determination to run away. The very first mental effort that I now remember on my part, was an attempt to solve the mystery, why am I a slave, and with this question my youthful mind was troubled for many days, pressing upon me more heavily at times than others. When I saw the slave-driver whip a slave woman, cut the blood out of her neck, and heard her piteous cries, I went away into the corner fence, wept, and pondered over the mystery. I had, through some medium, I know not what, got some idea of God, the Creator of all mankind, the black and the white, and that he had made the blacks to serve the whites as slaves. How he could do this and be good, I could not tell. I was not satisfied with this theory, which made God responsible for slavery, for it pained me greatly, and I have wept over it long and often. At one time, your first wife, Mrs. Lucretia, heard me singing and saw me shedding tears, and asked of me the matter, but I was afraid to tell her. I was puzzled with this question, till one night, while sitting in the kitchen, heard some of the old slaves talking of their parents having been stolen from Africa by white man, and were sold here as slaves. The whole mystery was solved at once. Very soon after this my aunt Jinny and uncle Noah ran away, and the great noise made about it by your father-in-law, made me for the first time acquainted with the fact, that there were free States as well as slave States. From that time, I resolved that I would some day run away. The morality of the act, I dispose as follows: I am myself; you are yourself; we are two distinct persons, equal persons. What you are, I am. You are a man, and so am I. God created both, and made us separate beings. I am not by nature bound to you, or you to me. Nature does not make your existence depend upon me, or mine to depend upon yours. I cannot walk upon your legs, or you upon mine. I cannot breathe for you, or you for me; I must breathe for myself, and you for yourself. We are distinct persons, and are each equally provided with faculties necessary to our individual existence. In leaving you, I took nothing but what belong to me, and in no way lessened your means for obtaining an honest living. . . .

Frederick Douglass

F. Scott Fitzgerald

In a more personal (as opposed to universal) vein, great writers and great historical figures are also individuals (naturally!) with families and personal lives. Fitzgerald, a famous American novelist (*The Great Gatsby, Tender Is the Night*), in August 1933 wrote some reflections to his daughter, Frances, who was away at camp:

Dear Pie:

All I believe in in life is the rewards for virtue (according to your talents) and the punishments for not fulfilling your duties, which are doubly costly. If there is such a volume in the camp library, will you ask Mrs. Tyson to let you look up a sonnet of Shakespeare's in which the line occurs, 'Lilies that fester smell far worse than weeds.'

. . . I will arrange the camp bill.

Half wit, I will conclude.

Things to worry about:
    Worry about courage
    Worry about cleanliness
    Worry about efficiency
    Worry about horsemanship
    Worry about . . .

Things not to worry about:
    Don't worry about popular opinion
    Don't worry about dolls
    Don't worry about the past
    Don't worry about the future
    Don't worry about growing up
    Don't worry about anybody getting ahead of you
    Don't worry about triumph
    Don't worry about failure unless it comes through
    your own fault
    Don't worry about mosquitoes
    Don't worry about flies
    Don't worry about insects in general
    Don't worry about parents
    Don't worry about boys
    Don't worry about disappointments
    Don't worry about pleasures
    Don't worry about satisfactions

Things to think about:
    What am I really aiming at?
    How good am I really in comparison to my contem-
    poraries in regard to:
    (a) Scholarship
    (b) Do I really understand about people and am I
         able to get along with them?
    (c) Am I trying to make my body a useful instru-
         ment or am I neglecting it?

With dearest love,
Daddy

Winston Churchill

Prime Minister of England during World War II,
Churchill is remembered as a courageous leader. His
speeches inspired the people of his country to keep
up their morale in the face of massive bombing at-

tacks from German planes sent by Adolf Hitler to conquer England. In 1940, he wrote (in part) to President Franklin D. Roosevelt as part of a long campaign to secure American support for the European war effort:

May 15, 1940

[Dear Mr. President:]

. . . As you are no doubt aware, the scene has darkened swiftly. The enemy have a marked preponderance in the air, and their new technique is making a deep impression upon the French.

I think myself the battle on land has only just begun, and I should like to see the masses engage. Up to the present, Hitler is working with specialized units in tanks and air.

The small countries are simply smashed up, one by one, like matchwood. We must expect, though it is not yet certain, that Mussolini will hurry in to share the loot of civilisation. We expected to be attacked here ourselves, both from the air and by parachute and air-borne troops in the near future, and are getting ready for them.

If necessary, we shall continue the war alone, and we are not afraid of that. But I trust you realise, Mr. President, that the voice and force of the United States may count for nothing if they are withheld too long. You may have a completely subjugated Nazified Europe established with astonishing swiftness, and the weight may be more than we can bear.

Groucho Marx

While some letters represent politics, government, and history on very serious levels, others are fun and entertaining. Famed comedian Groucho Marx, one of the Marx Brothers who worked together in vaudeville and in Hollywood films such as *A Night at the Opera* and *Room Service*, was a delightful writer. Groucho (it would be unnatural somehow to refer to him as "Marx") corresponded with many other famous people of his time, including other comedians, writers, publishers, and actors. This 1951 letter to comedian Fred Allen reflects Groucho's tongue-in-cheek style:

August 30, 1951

Dear Fred:

It is very difficult to correspond regularly with one who is not a woman. This, in case you care, explains why my letters are so infrequent. If, for example, one is corresponding with an attractive female—preferably not too old—there's always the likelihood that, at some future date you might be able to get closer to her. Corresponding with a man—a man our age, at any rate—soon reduces itself to a mutual cataloging of aches and pains, and the constant trials they are both being subjected to by the tax department.

Please don't assume from this that your letters are not worth receiving. The joy they give me can only be compared to the happiness I experienced years ago when a wire would arrive saying that we had received a year's booking on the Pantages Circuit [steady job in vaudeville]. I cherish each letter as though it were 'a gem of purest ray serene.' This, in case you care, is lifted from Thomas Gray and can be found on page 262 of Bartlett's Quotations.

My friend Goody [Ace, comedy writer] tells me that you're London-bound with the rowdy and predictable Tallulah [Bankhead, actor]. As one who has journeyed

on the high seas a number of times, I trust that you will
beware of card sharks, pool sharks, and in case you
should be lucky enough to fall overboard, just plain
sharks.

I wish I were going with you. What high old times we
could have—Goody, you, and I. Three old biddies
swapping aches and pains, telling tall tales of romantic
exploits and cursing television. Yes, Fred, we could
make the ship rock with our laughter.

So have a good time and my best to the Duchess.

Groucho

NOVELS MADE UP OF LETTERS

Many writers have used the form of letters to and
from various characters as the medium for a short
story or novel. An *epistolary novel* is one made up of
fictional letters. Using letters prompts the writer to express his or her thoughts in a conversational tone and
to organize the material so as to fit into letters while
keeping the plot moving along. Additionally, the
reader enjoys the feeling of being privileged to peek
into someone's private correspondence, even though
the individuals involved are characters of the imagi-
nation.

Jane Austen

Jane Austen was a writer in the 1800s whose witty,
finely detailed novels portrayed provincial English life.
In recent years several popular films based on her
novels have brought her work new attention. One of
her lesser-known works is *Lady Susan,* an epistolary

novella, or short novel, made up of letters to and from the title character. To appreciate Jane Austen's understanding of human passions, consider Lady Susan, a character who is a beautiful, hard-hearted, and manipulative woman. She would be a match for most of the scheming characters who are featured in "The Film of the Week" or the "real people" who appear on talk shows revealing how they have mistreated their families and friends. This is evident in a letter from Lady Susan (Mrs. Vernon) to her only friend, in which she discusses some communications between her own fiancé and her teenage daughter Frederica:

Mrs. Vernon to Mrs. Johnson

. . . I shall always detest them both. He can have no true regard for me, or he would not have listened to her; and she, with her little rebellious heart and indelicate feelings to throw herself into the protection of a young man with whom she had scarcely ever exchanged two words before. I am equally confounded at her impudence and his credulity. How dared he believe what she told him in my disfavour! Ought he not to have felt assured that I must have unanswerable motives for all that I had done! Where was his reliance on my sense or goodness then; where the resentment which true love would have dictated against the person defaming me, that person, too, a chit, a child, without talent or education, whom he had been always taught to despise?

I was calm for some time, but the greatest degree of forbearance may be overcome, and I hope I was afterwards sufficiently keen. He endeavoured, long endeavoured to soften my resentment, but that woman is a fool indeed who while insulted by accusation, can be worked on by compliments. At length he left me, as deeply provoked as myself, and he showed his anger more. I was quite cool, but he gave way to the most violent indignation. I may therefore expect it will sooner subside; and perhaps his may be vanished forever, while mine will be found still fresh and implacable.

He is now shut up in his apartment, whether I heard him go, on leaving mine. How unpleasant, one would think, must his reflections be! But some people's feelings are imcomprehensible. I have not yet tranquilized myself enough to see Frederica. She shall not soon forget the occurrences of this day. She shall find that she has poured forth her tender tale of love in vain, and exposed herself forever to the contempt of the whole world, and the severest resentment of her injured mother.

Yours affectionately,
S. Vernon

Gordon R. Dickson

Science fiction writer Gordon R. Dickson used the format of letters to tell a sinister tale in his 1965 short story "Computers Don't Argue." Some sci-fi writers love and embrace technology, and they use technological advances and their creative ideas about science, in their stories. Others, like Dickson in this story, paint a picture of technology out of control. Humans welcome and celebrate inventions that will make our lives easier, but then those devices can do things their inventors did not foresee, and machines end up ruling us.

Walter A. Child, the fictional main character, exchanges a series of letters with a book club that has been dunning him for money for a book he never received. Eventually, he gets a letter from an attorney and writes this reply in the hopes of ending the confusion:

437 Woodlawn Drive
Pandluk, Michigan
May 4, 1966

Mr. Hagthorpe M. Pruitt, Jr.
Maloney, Mahoney, MacNamara and Pruitt
89 Prince Street
Chicago, Illinois

Dear Mr. Pruitt:

You don't know what a pleasure it is to me in this matter to get a letter from a live human being to whom I can explain the situation.

This whole matter is silly. I explained it fully in my letters to the Treasure Book Company. But I might as well have been trying to explain to the computer that puts out their [bills], for all the good it seemed to do. Briefly, what happened was I ordered a copy of "Kim," by Rudyard Kipling for $4.98. When I opened the package they sent me, I found the book had only half its pages, but I'd previously mailed a check to pay them for the book.

I sent the book back to them, asking either for a whole copy or my money back. Instead, they sent me a copy of "Kidnapped," by Robert Louis Stevenson—which I had not ordered, and for which they have been trying to collect from me.

Meanwhile, I am still waiting for the money back that they owe me for the copy of "Kim" that I didn't get. That's the whole story. Maybe you can help me straighten them out.

Relievedly yours,
Walter A. Child

P.S. I also sent them back their copy of "Kidnapped," as soon as I got it, but it hasn't seemed to help. They have never even acknowledged getting it back.

Unfortunately, the law firm is not able to help, and the reference to Robert Louis Stevenson, famed author of *Kidnapped*, makes the situation worse. Computerized court records sent from Illinois to Michigan, where Child lives, are so garbled that he is accused and convicted of kidnapping and murdering Robert L. Stevenson! His lawyer understands that he is innocent and writes to the governor to try to get a pardon and forestall the death penalty. The governor responds appropriately, but bureaucracy—another common "enemy" in science fiction literature—and technology combine to stop the pardon. Presumably the execution goes forward, as the story ends with this chilling letter or memo (on the day of the planned execution):

Interdepartmental Routing Service

Failure to route Document properly.
To: Governor Hubert Daniel Willikens
Re: Pardon issued to Walter A. Child, July 1, 1966

Dear State Employee:

You have failed to attach your Routing Number.

PLEASE: Resubmit document with this card and form 876, explaining your authority for placing a TOP RUSH category on this document. Form 876 must be signed by your departmental supervisor.

RESUBMIT ON: Earliest possible date ROUTING SERVICE office is open. In this case, Tuesday, July 5, 1966.

WARNING: Failure to submit form 876 WITH THE SIGNATURE OF YOUR SUPERIOR may make you liable for prosecution for misusing a Service of the State Government. A warrant may be issued for your arrest.

There are NO exceptions. YOU have been WARNED.

Perhaps you can think of letters you have enjoyed reading, or have found memorable, either through history or literature. Letters are changing and evolving as are other types of communication, but letter writing is still a basic skill needed to "speak out and write on!"

APPENDIX

*T*ITLES AND SALUTATIONS: A QUICK REFERENCE

Occasionally you may want to or need to write to a person who deserves as a mark of respect a special title and salutation, other than the usual "Mr.," "Mrs.," "Miss," or "Ms." These are generally people with religious titles, those in political offices, or those in military offices. The following selected list of special titles was adapted with permission from *Webster's New Collegiate Dictionary* (Merriam-Webster). When more than one salutation is given, the first one is the more formal; if you know the person, you can choose the second, or more informal, salutation.

THE PERSON	FORM OF ADDRESS	SALUTATION
Clerical and religious orders		
archbishop	The Most Reverend Archbishop of _____ OR The Most Reverend Joe Jones Archbishop of _____	Your Excellency: Dear Archbishop Jones:
bishop, Catholic	The Most Reverend Joe Jones Bishop of _____	Your Excellency: Dear Bishop Jones:

THE PERSON	FORM OF ADDRESS	SALUTATION
bishop, Episcopal	The Right Reverend Joe Jones Bishop of _____	Right Reverend Sir: Dear Bishop Jones:
bishop, Protestant other	The Reverend Joe Jones	Reverend Sir: Dear Bishop Jones:
brother, Catholic	Brother Joe, S.J. [initials of order]	Dear Brother Joe:
brotherhood, Catholic, superior of	Brother Nick, S.J., Superior	Dear Brother Nick:
clergyman, Protestant	The Reverend Joe Jones OR The Reverend Dr. Joe Jones (if the person has a doctor's degree)	Dear Sir: Dear Mr. Smith: Dear Dr. Smith:
nun	Sister Mary Angelica, S.C.	Dear Sister Mary Angelica: Dear Sister:
patriarch (of Eastern church)	His Beatitude the Patriarch of _____	Most Reverend Lord:
pope	His Holiness Pope _____ OR His Holiness the Pope	Your Holiness: OR Most Holy Father:
priest	The Reverend Joe Jones OR The Reverend Father Jones	Dear Father Jones: Dear Father:
rabbi	Rabbi Joe Jones OR Rabbi Joe Jones, DD (if having a doctor's degree)	Dear Rabbi Jones: Dear Dr. Jones:

Diplomats

ambassador to US	His Excellency Joe Jones Ambassador of _____	Sir: Dear Mr. Ambassador:
American ambassador	The Honorable Joe Jones American Ambassador	Sir: Dear Mr. Ambassador:
chargé d'affaires, foreign	Ms. Jo Jones Chargé d'Affaires of _____	Madame: Dear Ms. Jones:

THE PERSON	FORM OF ADDRESS	SALUTATION
consul	Joe Jones, Esq.	Dear Sir:
secretary-general, UN	His Excellency Joe Jones Secretary-General of the United Nations	Excellency: Dear Mr. Secretary-General:

Government officials

THE PERSON	FORM OF ADDRESS	SALUTATION
alderman	The Honorable Joan Jones	Dear Ms. Jones:
assemblyman	See "representative, state"	
associate justice, Supreme Court	Mr. Justice Jones The Supreme Court of the United States	Sir: Dear Justice Jones:
cabinet officers	The Honorable Joe Jones Secretary of State	Dear Sir:
chief justice, Supreme Court	The Chief Justice of the United States	Dear Mr. Chief Justice:
governor	The Honorable Joan Jones Governor of _____	Dear Governor Jones:
judge, federal	The Honorable Joe Jones	Dear Judge Jones:
judge, state or local	The Honorable Joe Jones Chief Judge of the Court of Appeals	Dear Judge Jones:
mayor	The Honorable Joe Jones Mayor of _____	Dear Mayor Jones:
president, US	The President The White House	Mr. President: Dear Mr. President:
representative, state	The Honorable Joe Jones House of Representatives State Capitol	Dear Mr. Jones:
representative, US	The Honorable Joe Jones The United States House of Representatives	Sir: Dear Mr. Jones:

THE PERSON	FORM OF ADDRESS	SALUTATION
senator, state	The Honorable Joe Jones The State Senate State Capitol	Dear Senator Jones:
senator, US	The Honorable Joe Jones United States Senator	Dear Senator Jones:
vice-president, US	The Vice-President United States Senate	Dear Mr. Vice-President:

military ranks (a selected list)

admiral	(full rank plus full name plus a comma plus abbreviation of branch of service; example: Rear Admiral Joe Jones, USN [United States Navy])	Sir: Dear Admiral Smith:
cadet	Cadet Joe Jones United States Military Academy	Dear Cadet Jones:
captain (air force, army, coast guard, marine corps, or navy)	(full rank plus full name plus a comma plus abbreviation of branch of service)	Dear Captain Jones:
colonel or lieutenant colonel	(same as above)	Dear Colonel Jones:
commander (coast guard or navy)	(same as above)	Dear Commander Jones:
corporal	(same as above)	Dear Corporal Jones:
first lieutenant, second lieutenant (air force, army, or marine corps)	(same as above)	Dear Lieutenant Jones:
general, lieutenant general, major general	(same as above)	Sir: Dear General Jones:

THE PERSON	FORM OF ADDRESS	SALUTATION
major (air force, army, or marine corps)	(same as above)	Dear Major Jones:
midshipman	Midshipman Joe Jones United States Naval Academy	Dear Midshipman Jones:
petty officer and chief petty officer	(full rank plus full name plus comma plus branch of service)	Dear Mr. Jones: OR Dear Chief Jones:
private	(same as above)	Dear Private Smith:
other ranks	(same as above)	Dear + rank + last name:

Miscellaneous professions

attorney	Mr. Joe Jones Attorney-at-law OR Joe Jones, Esq.	Dear Mr. Jones:
dentist	Joan Jones, DDS (office address) OR Dr. Joan Jones (home address)	Dear Dr. Jones:
physician	Joe Jones, MD (office address) OR Dr. Joe Jones (home address)	Dear Dr. Jones:
professor, associate professor, assistant professor	(rank plus full name)	Dear + rank + last name:
veterinarian	Joe Jones, DVM (office address) OR Dr. Joe Jones (home address)	Dear Dr. Jones:

FOR MORE INFORMATION

For Further Reading

Ahmad, Nyla. *Cybersurfer: the Owl Internet Guide for Kids.* Toronto, Ont.: Owl Books (distributed in United States by Firefly books), 1996. Book plus computer disk.

The Associated Press Stylebook and Libel Manual. 6th trade ed. Reading, Mass.: Addison-Wesley, 1996.

The Chicago Manual of Style. 14th ed. Chicago: University of Chicago Press, 1993.

Clark, David. *Student's Guide to the Internet.* 2nd ed. Indianapolis, Ind.: Que Corporation, 1996.

Collin, Simon. *E-mail: A Practical Guide.* Oxford: Butterworth-Heinemann, 1995.

Farr, J. Michael. *The Quick Résumé & Cover Letter Book.* Indianapolis, Ind.: JIST Works, Inc., 1994.

Fein, Richard. *Cover Letters! Cover Letters! Cover Letters!* Hawthorne, N.J.: Book-Mart Press, 1994.

Gonyea, James C., and Wayne M. Gonyea. *Electronic Resumes: A Complete Guide to Putting your Resume Online.* New York: McGraw-Hill, 1995.

Kennedy, Joyce Lain. *Cover Letters for Dummies,* *2nd ed.* Foster City, Calif.: IDG Books Worldwide, 1998.

Li, Xia, and Nancy B. Crane. *Electronic Style: A Guide to Citing Electronic Information.* Westport, Conn.: Meckler, 1993.

Magid, Lawrence J. *Cruising Online: Larry Magid's Guide to the New Digital Highways.* New York: Random House Electronic Publishing, 1994.

Morris, Larry. *New Riders' Guide to E-mail and Messaging.* Indianapolis, Ind.: New Riders Publishing, 1994.

Occupational Outlook Handbook. Washington, D.C.: US Department of Labor, Bureau of Labor Statistics, US Government Printing Office, annual.

Standard & Poor's Register of Corporations, Directors, and Executives. New York: Standard & Poor's Corporation, annual.

Internet Sites

Due to the changeable nature of the Internet, sites appear and disappear very quickly. Internet addresses must be entered exactly as they appear.

The Yahoo directory of the World Wide Web is an excellent place to find Internet sites on any topic. The directory is located at: http://www.yahoo.com

Harnack, Andrew, and Gene Kleppinger. "Beyond the MLA Handbook: Documenting Electronic Sources on the Internet." http://falcon.eku.edu/honors/beyond-mla/

"Letter Writing." http://www.sasked.gov.sk.ca/docs/ela/ela_lett.html
An elementary introduction to letter writing as a way to communicate with others.

Lynch, Jack. "Grammar and Style Notes." http://www.english.upenn.edu/~jlynch/Grammar/

"Thank-You Letter Writing." http://www. american. edu/other.depts/career/thanku.htm
A guide to writing thank-letters after job interviews.

"Unforgettable Letters." http://www.usps.gov/letters/
An exploration of the power, humor, and drama of the written word.

"What is a Cover Letter?" http://www.american. edu/other.depts/career/coverlet.htm
Advice on writing cover letters to prospective employers.

"Writing a Complaint letter." http://www.pueblo.gsa. gov/1997crh/res_prt1.htm

"Writing Labs & Writing Centers on the Web." http://owl.english.purdue.edu/owls/writing
A website listing about 50 online writing sites offered by colleges and universities for all kinds of writing.

ACKNOWLEDGMENTS

The publishers listed here have generously given permission to use extended quotations from the following copyrighted works: From *Romantic Correspondence: Women, Politics, and the Fiction of Letters* by Mary A. Favret, copyright © 1993 by Cambridge University Press. Reprinted by permission of Cambridge University Press. From *The Mind of the Negro as Reflected in Letters Written During the Crisis: 1800-1860,* Carter G. Woodson, ed. Copyright © 1926 by The Association for the Study of Negro Life and History, Inc. Reprinted by permission of Reprint Services Corp. From *The Letters of F. Scott Fitzgerald.* Reprinted by permission of Scribner/ Simon and Schuster, Inc. From *Love Anyhow: Famous Fathers Write to their Children,* Reid Sherline, ed. Copyright © 1994 by Reid Sherline. Reprinted by permission of Harold Ober Associates, Inc. From *Winston S. Churchill,* vol. 3, Martin Gilbert, ed. Copyright © 1983 by C & T Publications Ltd. Reprinted by permission of Houghton Mifflin Co. From *The Groucho Letters* by Groucho Marx. Copyright © 1967 by Groucho Marx. Reprinted by permission of Simon and Schuster, Inc. From *Merriam-Webster's Collegiate® Dictionary,* 10th ed. Copyright © 1997 by Merriam-Webster, Inc. Reprinted by permission of Merriam-Webster, Inc.

$\mathscr{I}$NDEX

ABOUT THE
AUTHOR

Patricia Dragisic has worked as an editor and writer for more than twenty-five years in reference book publishing in Chicago. She has also edited English textbooks for the high school and college levels. During her career, she has corresponded with numerous publishers, writers, editors, professors, artists, and others. A graduate of Northwestern University's Medill School of Journalism, she is a longtime volunteer at the Chicago Public Library. In her spare time she writes letters to the editor (she's had dozens published in various newspapers) and to her elected representatives.